Turning
Vintage Toys

You'll just love making these wonderful toys!

Turning
Vintage Toys

CHRIS REID

GUILD OF MASTER
CRAFTSMAN PUBLICATIONS

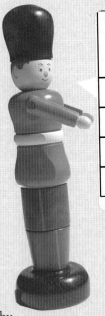

First published 2009 by
Guild of Master Craftsman
Publications Ltd
Castle Place, 166 High Street,
Lewes, East Sussex BN7 1XU

ISBN 978–1–86108–602–0

Associate Publisher: Jonathan Bailey
Production Manager: Jim Bulley
Managing Editor: Gerrie Purcell
Managing Art Editor: Gilda Pacitti
Editors: Mark Bentley & Beth Wicks
Designers: Rebecca Mothersole and
         Chris & Jane Lanaway
Photographer: Anthony Bailey
Illustrator: Chris Reid

Set in Abode Garamond, Gill Sans,
Myriad, Fiesta, Ribbon, and Didot

Colour origination by
GMC Reprographics

Printed and bound by Kyodo Nation
Printing in Thailand

Measurements
All the projects are measured in both
inches and millimeters. When following
the projects, use either the metric or
imperial; do not mix units.

Safety Notice
When making toys for children be
aware of both choking hazards and
sharp points. For more information
refer to the toy safety legislation or
appropriate legislation for your country.

Please note: these designs are not
intended for commercial purposes.

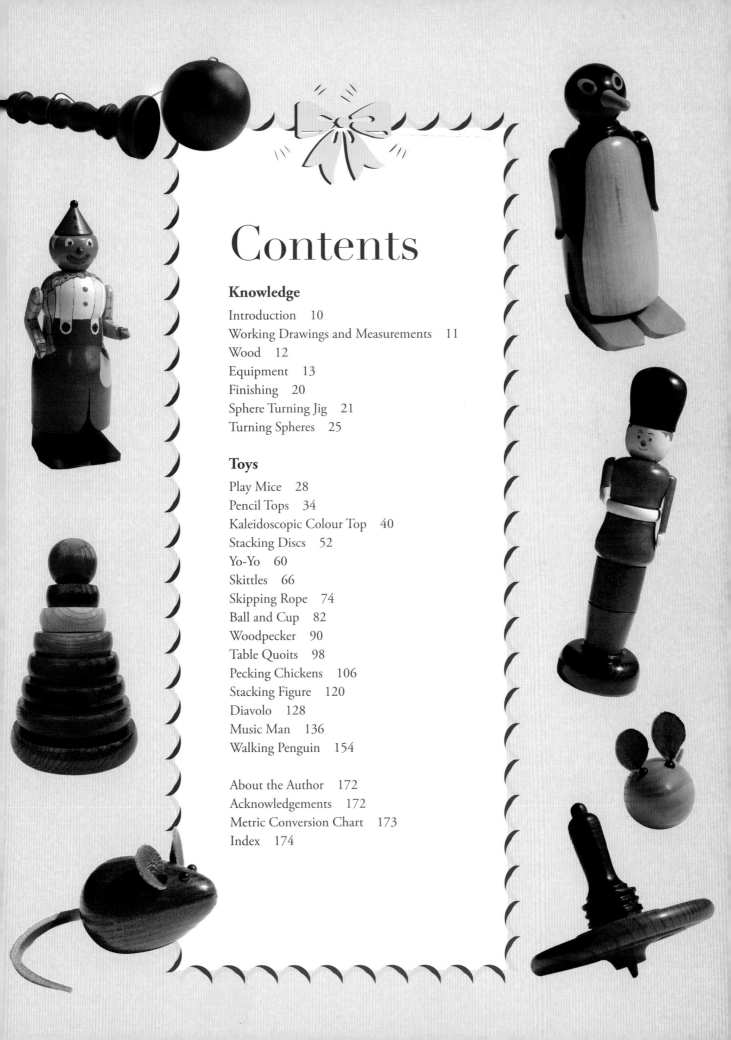

Contents

A wide range of beautiful, wooden toys, perfect for both the beginner and expert wood turner. I'm on page 154.

Introduction

This book is not about how to turn wood, but instead to give you an idea of the basic requirements for the turning and assembly of specific toys. Even the fact that they are made of wood can be lost, unless you want to construct the pieces from exotic or colourful timbers which are then polished or finished to display their beauty.

As a turner of wood I prefer this type of finish, but you can make the choice for yourself, the possibilities are almost endless. The main thing is to enjoy your woodturning, whatever shape or direction it takes.

PREPARATION OF BLANKS

All the projects begin with a cutting list, which includes all the items that are necessary to complete the toy. Unless stated otherwise, the blanks are sawn square, that is with edges at 90° to each other. Where the item requires holes to be at right angles to one another, the operation can be carried out on the drill press very simply ad accurately.

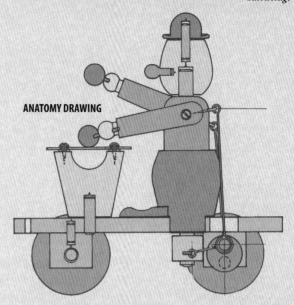

ANATOMY DRAWING

Working Drawings and Measurements

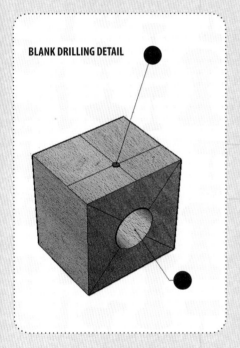

BLANK DRILLING DETAIL

All the measurements in the drawings and text are in both imperial and metric, with the exception of hand chased threads which are measured in threads per inch. **The conversions are approximate**. To convert millimetres to inches, multiply by 0.03937.

The working drawings are divided into three different categories and have been produced like this to maintain clarity.

ANATOMY DRAWINGS

These are coloured drawings and show the main points for the assembly of the toy. Where the details are simple, requiring few dimensions, these are included in the anatomy drawing.

BLANK DRILLING DETAIL

These drawings are perspective drawings of the prepared blanks. That is, blanks cut to size from the details shown in the relevant cutting list. Each one shows the marking out and drilling of the blank prior to mounting on the lathe or gluing into composite blanks.

DETAIL DRAWINGS

The drawings under this category show all the relevant details and dimensions for the finished item. Where dimensions are repeated from the blank drilling detail, for example hole centres or sizes of holes, these are shown in italics as references. The aim is to keep the plans as simple as possible so following them in the workshop is straightforward.

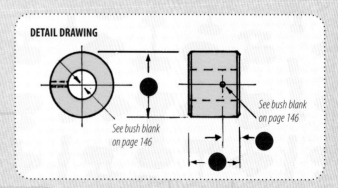

DETAIL DRAWING

See bush blank on page 146

See bush blank on page 146

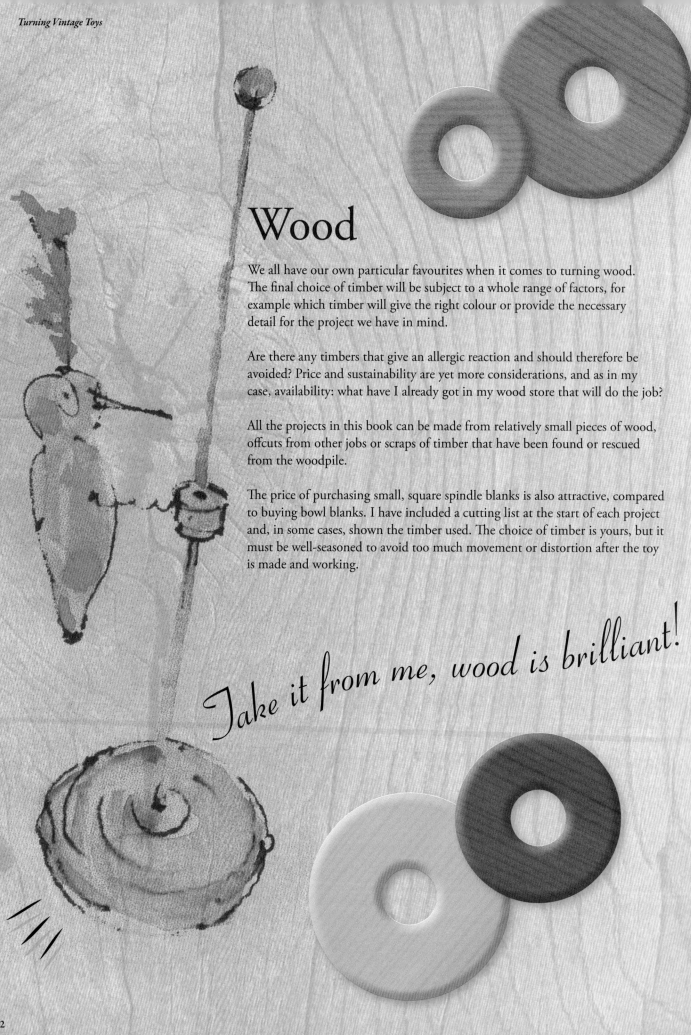

Wood

We all have our own particular favourites when it comes to turning wood. The final choice of timber will be subject to a whole range of factors, for example which timber will give the right colour or provide the necessary detail for the project we have in mind.

Are there any timbers that give an allergic reaction and should therefore be avoided? Price and sustainability are yet more considerations, and as in my case, availability: what have I already got in my wood store that will do the job?

All the projects in this book can be made from relatively small pieces of wood, offcuts from other jobs or scraps of timber that have been found or rescued from the woodpile.

The price of purchasing small, square spindle blanks is also attractive, compared to buying bowl blanks. I have included a cutting list at the start of each project and, in some cases, shown the timber used. The choice of timber is yours, but it must be well-seasoned to avoid too much movement or distortion after the toy is made and working.

Take it from me, wood is brilliant!

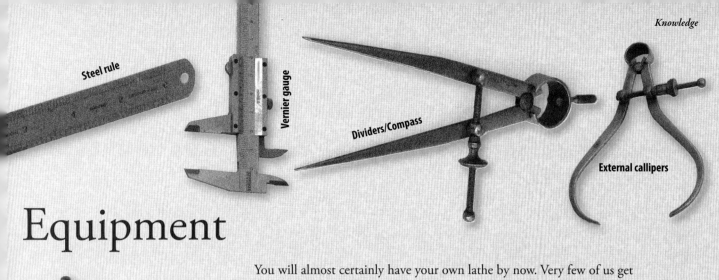

Steel rule

Vernier gauge

Dividers/Compass

External callipers

Equipment

Pencil compass

You will almost certainly have your own lathe by now. Very few of us get the choice of lathe right the first time and as our experience grows and the direction of what we want to turn changes so do the requirements of the lathe. Size and price will probably determine your choice as much as technical specifications. There are plenty of books, DVDs and informative woodturning magazines which give good, impartial advice. Professional turners are usually more than willing to pass on their expert knowledge. Courses and clubs are a great way of trying different lathes and tools, so you will never be stuck for choice. Keep your lathe in good order by regular maintenance. The banjo, tool rest and tailstock quill should all move with the lightest of touches and be easy to lock positively. Test the alignment of tailstock and headstock centre points regularly.

In addition to the essential lathe, woodturners usually acquire a range of equipment and tools related to their own specialization. The items below are useful additions to a workshop and will make the production of these toys easier.

BAND SAW

Not absolutely essential, but this is a very handy piece of equipment. A small bench model with a depth of cut of 4in (100mm) should cover all the projects in this book. However, like the lathe, do not restrict yourself to only what you will need for these projects. An 8in (200mm) minimum depth of cut should serve you well and allow some diversity in the future.

MARKING & MEASURING EQUIPMENT

A typical woodturner's range of tools is shown above and below. A small vernier calliper will be useful. The bradawl is sharpened to a three-sided point, so it acts like a reamer to remove the wood rather than just indent a hole.

Bradawl

Internal callipers

Square

Pencil

HOLDING JIGS

BENCH OR PILLAR DRILL

Accurate drilling operations are relatively simple and can be carried out on even the most basic of bench drills. Certainly nothing very sophisticated is necessary to complete any of the projects in this book. A machine that can drill an accurate hole at 90° to the drill table is all that is required.

Yet there are some safety considerations, mainly concerning the holding of objects. A large drill diameter in a relatively small work piece can potentially cause a serious injury. There are two simple ways to overcome this. One is to loosen the belt drive to a point where the drill bit will stop if it jams, but a better way is to ensure that the item being drilled is held securely in a clamp or jig. A simple jig is shown in the drawing below and is quick and simple to use **1**.

Another jig used throughout the book is for holding objects after they have been turned. Round profiles are not a problem, these can be held in a vee-block quite safely. Spherical items, however, need a special solution. The answer is to make a number of small flat discs or squares with a hole just a bit smaller than the profile being drilled **2**. A number of these can be made and kept ready to use.

TYPES OF HOLDING JIG

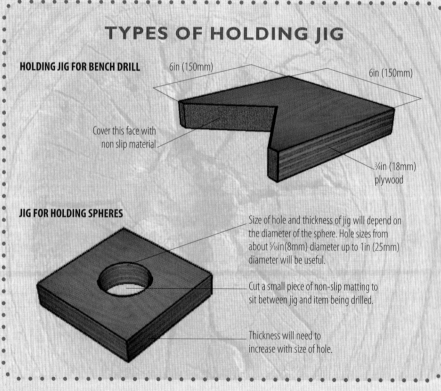

HOLDING JIG FOR BENCH DRILL

6in (150mm)

6in (150mm)

Cover this face with non slip material

¾in (18mm) plywood

JIG FOR HOLDING SPHERES

Size of hole and thickness of jig will depend on the diameter of the sphere. Hole sizes from about ⁵⁄₁₆in (8mm) diameter up to 1in (25mm) diameter will be useful.

Cut a small piece of non-slip matting to sit between jig and item being drilled.

Thickness will need to increase with size of hole.

Always keep your beak, oops sorry I mean tools, sharp!

Yes, and keep your mind sharp too!

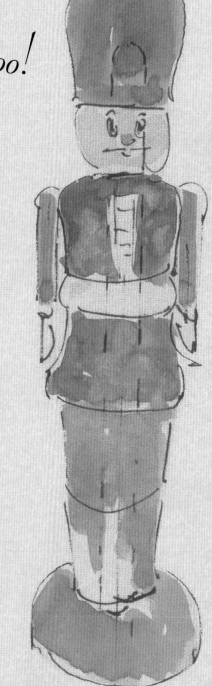

SANDING DISC

The ability to sand items against a flat surface is a great asset for all sorts of items, from furniture to segmented bowls, and will be essential for the production of the walking toys.

A shopbuilt attachment for the lathe may prove to be invaluable. Making one machine do several jobs is also a good way of saving space in a small workshop.

SHARPENING

We become so used to using power tools that we tend to forget that woodturning is just a form of using hand tools, chisels and gouges. When these tools cease to cut efficiently, we lose much of the pleasure and our creative ability.

One of the elementary rules of using any hand tool is to let the tool do the work. This simply means keeping it sharp and using it only for its intended purpose. No chisel or gouge can be used effectively or with pleasure unless it is sharp. A firm grip may force the tool along its way, but it will behave unpredictably and dangerously, whereas a sharp edge is vital for true workmanship and artistic achievement.

Make sharpening an essential and regular routine at the start of every job. The harder the wood, the more you will need to sharpen. Whatever method you use, it must be readily and easily achievable, preferably only needing a step or two from the lathe to the stone. There are many really good commercial jigs to help you keep a consistent shape to your edges, plus it's almost impossible to overheat modern sintered tools.

Mini collet chuck

Scrap wood spigot chucks

CHUCKS & ACCESSORIES

Scroll or geared chucks are one of the best advances in recent years, consisting of a key operated mechanism which moves the jaws to grip the work piece. The jaws are double-sided so they can work in compression or expansion mode. Most will be supplied with a 2in (50mm) set of jaws. An additional set of 1in (25mm) jaws would be useful for the projects here. A screw chuck is also usually supplied with the basic chuck. If your lathe does not have an indexing facility, choosing a chuck and index arm can add this useful feature to your lathe.

Jacobs-type chucks, fitted with Morse tapers to suit your head and tailstock spindles, are ideal for drilling on the lathe or for holding small pieces of wood. Their only drawback is that they will not accommodate square stock. A recent accessory to the market are collet chucks. These are incredibly accurate and will hold square or round stock from ³⁄₆₄in (1mm) to about ¹⁹⁄₃₂in (15mm), at which point the smaller scroll chucks take over. For their price and precision, these little chucks are not worth trying to make.

A two or four pronged driving spur is essential for any between centres work. Multi-spur drives are a useful addition to your drive accessories and are available in various sizes. Their advantage is the spring loaded centre point, which reduces the need to drive in the spurs with a mallet as with the older types.

A live (revolving) centre in the tailstock has replaced the old type of dead centre which burnt the wood. A very useful accessory you can make is a live centre cup.

2in (50mm) Scroll chuck and key

Multi-spur drives

4 Spur drives

Standard live centre

Live centre cup

Jacobs chuck

1in (25mm) Jaw set

Collet chuck

CUP

LIVE CENTRE CUP

1 Mount the blank directly into the jaws of your expansion chuck and square up the end. Drill a hole to suit the diameter of your live centre x 1³⁄₁₆in (30mm) deep. The live centre should be a nice sliding fit with very little play. Drill a ⁵⁄₈in (15mm) diameter hole through the blank on the same centre. Apply some sanding sealer inside the hole to stabilize the timber.

2 Reverse mount onto a spigot or small expanding chuck and square up the face. Rough down the blank to a 1¾in (45mm) diameter cylinder.

3 Cut a recess to accommodate the O-ring **1**. The depth needs to be just over half the thickness of the O-ring. Turn a small radius on the outside edge of the cup. Form a 45° chamfer between the inside of the ring to the hole **2**. Sand and seal the whole jig and fit the O-ring. This little jig is a very handy addition to your lathe tools and is used several times throughout the book.

MATERIALS

- Hardwood blank 1³¹⁄₃₂in x 1³¹⁄₃₂in x 2¾in (50mm x 50mm x 70mm) long
- 1³⁄₃₂in (28mm) inside diameter O-ring.
- The size of O-ring is approximate. You can make any number of these cups with varying sizes of rings to suit other applications.

SPIGOT CHUCKS

Many of the projects use a simple spigot-type chuck which you need to make yourself; these are sacrificial and use scraps of timber. They are, of course, held in your standard scroll chuck.

Two types of spigot chuck are made, the relevant details are shown below.

Button plates or cole jaws are useful for finishing the reverse side of discs to clean up the dovetail recess or spigot. If you are adept at making jam chucks, these work just as well, but need to be made specifically for each job.

TYPES OF SPIGOT CHUCK

STANDARD SPIGOT CHUCK

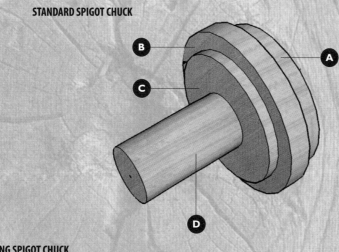

EXPANDING SPIGOT CHUCK

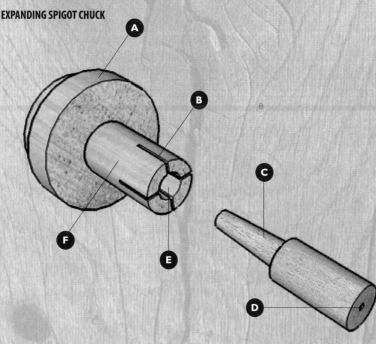

STANDARD SPIGOT CHUCK

A Dovetail spigot to match your own chuck

B 1³¹⁄₃₂in (50mm) diameter x ¹³⁄₃₂in (10mm)

C 1³⁄₁₆in (30mm) diameter x ³⁄₁₆in (5mm)

D Diameter and length to suit item being turned

EXPANDING SPIGOT CHUCK

A 1³¹⁄₃₂in (50mm) diameter x ¹³⁄₃₂in (10mm) approx

B 4 x saw cuts at 90° spacing x ³⁄₄in (20mm) long

C ³¹⁄₃₂in (25mm) long plug tapering ¹¹⁄₃₂in (9mm) diameter to ¹⁵⁄₃₂in (12mm) diameter

D Tailstock centre

E ³⁄₈in (10mm) diameter hole drilled through centre of chuck to allow knocking out of plug if necessary

F Diameter and length to suit item being tuned

HAND TOOLS

We probably all go to shows or demonstrations and become convinced that a particular chisel or gouge is essential to improve our technique. Some are just gimmicks, while others prove to be invaluable. I only ever use half the number of tools I once thought were absolutely vital, but they all look very nice hanging on the wall.

The list of tools required for the projects here consist of:

¹⁄₁₆in (1 ½mm) + ⅛in (3mm) parting tools

⅜in (10mm) and ⅝in (16mm) bowl gouge

Straight and round edge scrapers in various sizes

16 + 20 tpi (threads per inch) thread chasers and recess tool

A recently purchased ring cutter (not a gimmick!)

⅜in (10mm) detail chisel

¾in (19mm) skew chisel

¼in (6mm) + ⅜in (10mm) spindle gouges

Roughing gouge

Small three-point tool

Chatter tool

The ⅜in (10mm) detail chisel is my general purpose tool, used for planing, cutting dovetails, beads and many other cuts. The recess tool is made from an old carbon steel chisel and cuts a ⁵⁄₆₄in (2mm) recess at the bottom of internal threads. The scrapers are in different shapes and sizes to suit the job in hand. A particularly useful one is ground to cut dovetail recesses.

The ring cutter has several different sized cutters which can all be purchased individually as finances allow. It is not essential, but makes the production of rings very simple and saves a tremendous amount of time, as well as timber.

ABRASIVES

Most sanding on the lathe is done by hand and abrasive paper is just another cutting tool. Try to get the best possible finish from the tool first and slow the lathe speed down to a maximum of 700rpm.

Cloth-backed, resin-bonded aluminium oxide takes some beating, but you must work through the grades in order. Depending on the timber and the finish you can achieve straight from the chisel, start with the coarsest grit necessary. The grits start at 60, but you should not really need anything this coarse.

The normal range is 120, 150, 180, 240, 320 and 400, going on to 600, 800, 1200 and 1500 for an ultra fine surface. When used in order, each grade should remove the scratches from the previous paper.

Two points to remember; firstly, sanding will generate a lot of heat. Many timbers are prone to heat checks, tiny cracks that are often not visible until the finish is applied. Do not fold the paper into double or triple thickness. The exception to this rule is when there are openings or holes in the blank and you need the additional thickness for protection. A single thickness will allow you to feel the temperature you are generating and ease off. If it's too hot for your finger, it's certainly too hot for the timber.

Secondly, this abrasive is friable, so tiny pieces of grit can break off to reveal new sharp edges. These pieces can often remain on the surface of the freshly sanded work. Moving straight on to the next finer grade will pick up this larger grit and take all your work back a stage. Use a tack rag or dampened cloth between each stage to achieve the best result in the shortest time.

Finishing

The type of finish needs careful consideration at the outset. It determines the treatment of the blank while still on the lathe. Sanding need only be taken to 320 grit if the item is to be painted, whereas a much finer abrasive will be required if a polished finish is sought.

Sanding sealers also need to be chosen in relation to the finish. Cellulose sealers contain chalk and will leave tiny white deposits in the grain of timber. This is all right on light coloured wood, but may spoil the appearance of the darker timbers. Most of the projects in the book require the application of a sanding sealer to seal and stabilize the wood and also to provide a good foundation for the final finish or paint.

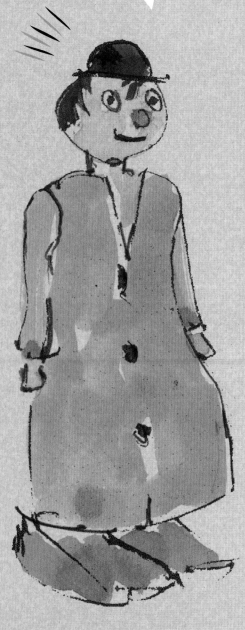

WARNING

Whatever finish you choose must be food or toy safe and marked to conform with the appropriate legislation of your country.

Sphere Turning Jig

A few of the projects in this book require the turning of one or more spheres. You may find that a jig to help get perfect spheres is a useful addition to your own workshop. Commercial jigs are available, but if you enjoy making your own, the following example is fairly straightforward and requires only basic engineering skills.

SOURCING THE MATERIALS

Before starting to make the jig, there are some important considerations to think about regarding the method of fitting the jig to your own lathe and possible adjustments to the sizes given below in relation to your individual circumstances. The basic version of the jig fits into the tool post holder on the banjo. It is not tightened as the tool rest would be, but is free to rotate, using the post hole as a pivot point. The G-clamp chosen must therefore have a thread diameter no greater than your tool post unless you have the facility to machine it to suit. The second important measurement to consider is the distance between the top face of the tool post hole and the drive axis of the lathe.

The minimum dimension here needs to be about 3in (75mm) to accommodate the largest sphere in the book. If the swing of your lathe is less than this, fit the pivot directly to the bed of your lathe on a small saddle or clamp, see the drawing on page 22. Once satisfied that the minimum requirements can be met, you can start to make the jig.

MATERIALS

- Heavy duty type G-clamp about 8in (200mm) x 3½in (90mm)

- 1³⁄₁₆in (30mm) wide x ⁵⁄₃₂in (4mm) thick x 4¾in (120mm) long mild steel strip (makes two plates)

- ³⁄₁₆in (5mm) bolts x 1in (25mm) long, plus nuts and washers (two required)

- ³⁄₁₆in (5mm) bolt x 1³⁄₁₆in (30mm) long plus ³⁄₁₆in (5mm) threaded cross dowel (the type used in flat pack furniture)

- 1⁹⁄₁₆in (40mm) length of ⁵⁄₁₆in (8mm) studding (you can cut the head off a 1⁹⁄₁₆in (40mm) long bolt)

- 1⁹⁄₁₆in (40mm) x 1¹⁹⁄₁₆in (40mm) x ⁵⁄₈in (15mm) thick plywood blank and ⁵⁄₁₆in (8mm) thread insert or hexagon nut

- 1¹⁄₁₆in (27mm) x 1¹⁄₁₆in (27mm) x 4¾in (120mm) long piece of hardwood

- ⅛in (3mm) diameter x 1in (25mm) long spring steel roll pin

- ⅜in (10mm) square cobalt steel tool bit x 4in (100mm) long (used in metal working lathes)

- ³⁄₁₆in (5mm) diameter steel washers, as required

SPHERE TURNING JIG

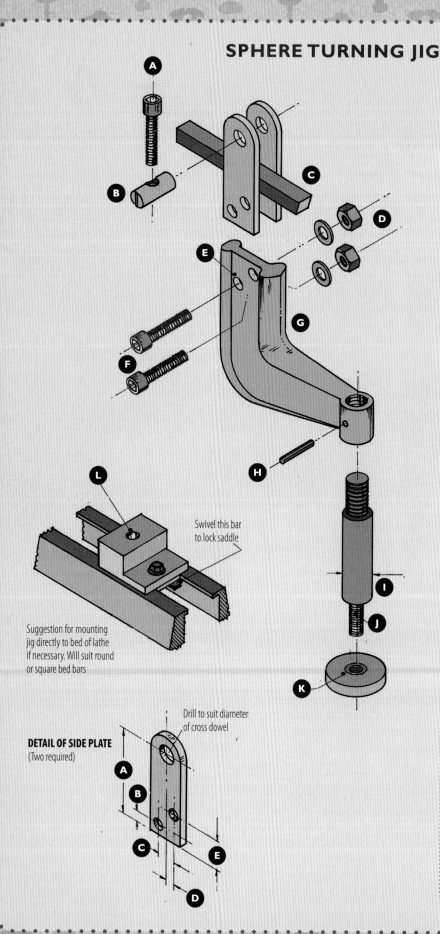

Suggestion for mounting jig directly to bed of lathe if necessary. Will suit round or square bed bars

Swivel this bar to lock saddle

Drill to suit diameter of cross dowel

DETAIL OF SIDE PLATE
(Two required)

NOTES ON CUTTERS

Sharpen the cutter straight across with a rake of approximately 10°.

The cutter illustrated can easily be changed for a bedan or shear cutter. Whatever tool is used, adjustment will be required to ensure that the cutting height is the same as the drive axis.

A handled tool provides excellent control, but make sure that the handle does not impede the full swing of the jig.

SPHERE TURNING JIG

A ³⁄₁₆in (5mm) x 1³⁄₁₆in (30mm) long cap head bolt

B Cross dowel

C ³⁄₈in (10mm) square tool bit

D ³⁄₁₆in (5mm) nuts & washers

E Fit ³⁄₁₆in (5mm) diameter washers to adjust width for cutter

F ³⁄₁₆in (5mm) x 1³⁄₁₆in (30mm) long cap head bolts

G 8in (200mm) x 3½in (90mm) heavy duty G clamp

H ⅛in (3mm) diameter roll pin to lock tool post

I Diameter to suit your tool post

J ⁵⁄₁₆in (8mm) diameter thread

K ⁵⁄₁₆in (8mm) thread insert in centring disc

L Drill this hole to suit the diameter of the G clamp threaded rod. Drill on exact centre of drive axis

SIDE PLATE

A 1¾in (45mm)

B ³⁄₈in (9mm)

C ½in (13mm)

D ¼in (6.5mm)

E ⁵⁄₈in (16mm)

MAKING THE JIG

1 Unscrew the threaded rod from the clamp. This will mean cutting the end swivel off.

2 Accurately measure the distance from the top of the tool post hole to the drive axis of your lathe. Using this measurement, subtract the thickness of the tool steel cutter. Mark a line across the body of the clamp, measuring from the bottom of the threaded hole. Use a hacksaw to cut a straight and square edge across the body. Accuracy here will mean that the jig will automatically cut the sphere at the centre point of the blank every time it is fitted.

3 Mark out and drill the two plates as detailed in the drawing opposite. Some filing and shaping will be necessary to ensure the plates fit nicely inside the cast web of the clamp.

4 Drill the two holes in the clamp and fit the plates **1**. Use washers each side as necessary to give just enough width inside the plates to allow the removal of the tool bit without too much lateral movement.

5 Measure the distance from the top of the tool post hole to the lathe bed and add on ⅛in (3mm) for clearance. Screw the threaded rod into the clamp until the cut end is flush with the top of the threaded hole. Cut the exposed portion of rod to the length you have just measured.

6 Unscrew the rod and mount in the jaws of your chuck. Fit a Jacobs-type chuck in the tailstock and use a centre drill or ⅛in (3mm) diameter high speed twist drill to make a pilot hole in the centre of the rod **2a**. Drill a ⁵⁄₁₆in (8mm) x 1in (25mm) deep tapping hole and use an engineer's tap to cut a ⁵⁄₁₆in (8mm) thread **2b**. See Top Tip.

JIG

1

2a

2b

TOP TIP

If you are not confident with this process, you can drill a ⁵⁄₁₆in (8mm) diameter clearance hole and glue the stud into the rod using an epoxy resin.

FITTING THE JIG

The following procedure is only necessary if the diameter of the threaded rod on the G-clamp is smaller than your tool post diameter.

1 Cut the hardwood blank to the length measured in step 5 on page 23. Drill the blank to suit the diameter of the threaded rod **1**. Glue the blank onto the rod.

2 Mount the rod in the chuck and rough down to a cylinder. Use a skew chisel to plane the surface to the required diameter to give a nice sliding fit in your tool post holder **2**. Apply a couple of coats of sanding sealer.

3 Screw the rod back into the clamp body and drill a cross hole to fit the roll pin **3**.

CENTRING PLATE

1 Mark the diagonals on one face of the blank. Drill a hole through the centre to accommodate the ⁵⁄₁₆in (8mm) threaded insert. Press in the insert.

2 Cut off the corners to help turning if necessary and mount the blank on a mandrel. Turn down to match the inside dimension of your lathe bed. Allow a small clearance for fitting. This disc will ensure that the centre point of the tool post (pivot point of the jig) is vertically in line with the axis of the blank every time the jig is fitted. All the parts are ready for assembly **1a** and the assembled jig is ready for action **1b**. See following section on turning spheres.

TOOL POST

CENTRING PLATE

Cutting List

To make a 2¾in (70mm) diameter sphere using the jig.

SPHERE

2¹⁵⁄₁₆in x 2¹⁵⁄₁₆in x 3¾in
(75mm x 75mm x 95mm) long

DRIVE CUP

3¹⁷⁄₃₂in x 3¹⁷⁄₃₂in x 1³¹⁄₃₂in
(90mm x 90mm x 50mm) long

You will also need a 2in (50mm) faceplate ring.

Turning Spheres

1   Mark the diagonals on each end of the sphere blank and make an indent with the point of a bradawl. Mount the blank between centres.

2   Rough down the blank to a diameter of 2¾in (70mm). Mark a line in pencil around the centre and two more lines at 1⅜in (35mm) each side of the centre. Use a parting tool to cut two ¾in (20mm) diameter spigots from the outer lines to the ends of the blank, leaving a centrally positioned cylinder 2¾in (70mm) diameter x 2¾in (70mm) wide **1**.

3   Set up the jig with the cutting edge of the tool bit at the axis of the drive centre. Fit the centring disc to bring the centre of the swing of the jig vertically in line with the drive axis.

4   Loosen the cutter and the banjo and adjust both to the point where the cutter just touches the two corners of the cylinder when swung from left to right **2**. Tighten the banjo.

5   Swing the jig back to the central position and adjust the cutter to take a light cut equally across both corners. Fully tighten the bolt to ensure the cutter is secure.

6   Switch on the lathe and, holding the jig, slowly swing it to the left, cutting a small section from the corner of the blank. Now swing the jig over to the right corner and cut this area **3**. Return the jig to the central position and switch off the lathe.

7   Adjust the cutter in towards the blank so it will take a slightly deeper cut and repeat the procedure, cutting from left to right and back to centre. Turn off the lathe before adjusting the cutter. Repeat this procedure as many times as necessary, taking only light cuts, until the final cut has just left the pencil line intact **4**. You can remove the cutter easily to sharpen it at any time.

8   When the final cut has been made, remove the jig and sand the profile. Cut off the stubs leaving ¼in (5–6mm) at either side.

TURNING SPHERES

DRIVE CUP

This driving jig is necessary to finish turning the sphere and is used in conjunction with the live centre cup described on page 17.

1 Mark the centre on one end grain of the blank and fit a faceplate ring. Mount on to your expansion chuck.

2 Turn the blank down to a diameter to suit the faceplate ring and cut or drill a 1⅜in (35mm) diameter hole x ⅝in (16mm) deep in the face of the blank. Chamfer the edge of the hole at 45° to accept and hold the sphere **1a**.

3 Chamfer the outside profile to give a bit of clearance when the sphere is in position, but leave sufficient material around the inner chamfer to support the sphere **1b**. Make a reference mark on the edge of the faceplate to enable remounting of the jig as accurately as possible in the future **1c**.

FINISHING THE SPHERE

1 Fit the tailstock cover onto the live centre. Then with the holding jig still on the headstock, place the part turned sphere between centres with the stubs at approximately 90° to their original axis.

2 Position the tool rest to clear the stubs, rotating by hand before switching on the lathe to check. Use a small gouge to turn away the stubs to leave a perfect sphere. Sand to match the rest of the profile then remove from the lathe **2**.

DRIVE CUP & SPHERE

1a

1b

1c

2

Our motto is: be ready for anything!

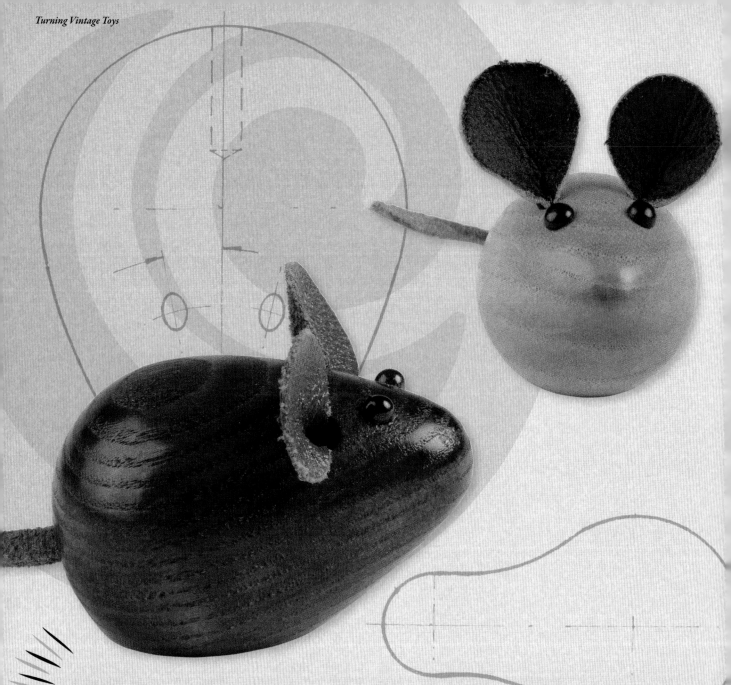

PLAY MICE

This mouse was never intended to be a toy. Some years ago, I made some as a bit of fun to turn and to test some water-based stains. Having made several, in all colours, I placed them around the workshop and on various window sills in the house to see how permanent the colours would be.

Well, the children loved them and soon wanted more.

I have made quite a few since and never have a problem giving them away.

So what colours are the most permanent? I don't know.

All those mice have long since disappeared into toy boxes or into children's bedrooms.

Cutting List

1 piece 1⁹⁄₁₆in x 1⁹⁄₁₆in x 2¹¹⁄₃₂in
(40mm x 40mm x 60mm) long

The choice of timber is yours. I have chosen a piece of ash (*Fraxinus excelsior*) because it stains well which younger children like, and still shows the grain which older children seem to prefer.

In addition to the above, you will need some ⁵⁄₃₂in (4mm) diameter black dowel for the eyes, a thin piece of leather for the ears and a 2⁹⁄₁₆in (65mm) length of leather shoelace for the tail.

ANATOMY DRAWING OF PLAY MICE

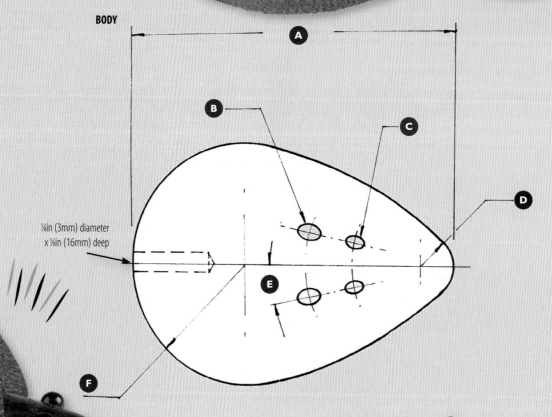

BODY

⅛in (3mm) diameter
x ⅝in (16mm) deep

EYE PROFILE

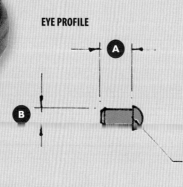

EAR PROFILE

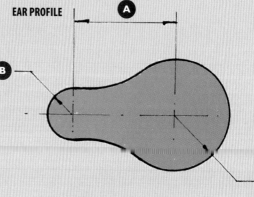

BODY

A 2in (50mm)

B ⁵⁄₃₂in (4mm) diameter
x ¹³⁄₃₂in (10mm) deep

C ⅛in (3mm) diameter
x ¼in (6mm) deep

D ³⁄₁₆in (5mm) radius

E 30°

F ²³⁄₃₂in (18mm) radius

EYE PROFILE

A ³⁄₁₆in (5mm)

B ⅛in (3mm)

C ⁵⁄₆₄in (2mm) radius

EAR PROFILE

A ¹⁹⁄₃₂in (15mm) centres

B ⁵⁄₃₂in (4mm) radius

C ⁵⁄₁₆in (8mm) radius

BODY

1 Mark the diagonals on the end grain and make a small indent on the centre point, this can be done using a bradawl **1** . The advantage with marking centres this way is that the consequent mounting or drilling operation is much easier and will be more accurate.

2 Drill a ⅛in (3mm) diameter hole x ⅝in (16mm) deep into the centre mark at one end **2** .

3 Mount between centres using a small 4-prong drive at the headstock end and the tailstock live centre in the ⅛in (3mm) diameter hole.

4 Using a roughing gouge, turn the blank down to a cylinder, just removing any flat surfaces **3a** . Square up the tailstock end with a parting tool **3b** . Mark a pencil line around the blank at half the diameter from the tailstock end **3c** .

5 Turn a radius on the tailstock end. Use the pencil line as a reference point for the centre of your radiused end and try to form the curve in a uniform manner, removing wood evenly on both the front and end surfaces. Use a template if necessary to check that you are turning a nice smooth radius **4** .

TOP TIP

Sharpen your chisel, even if you think it is sharp, before taking a final light cut over the whole profile. Keep the bevel rubbing behind the cut to polish the surface.

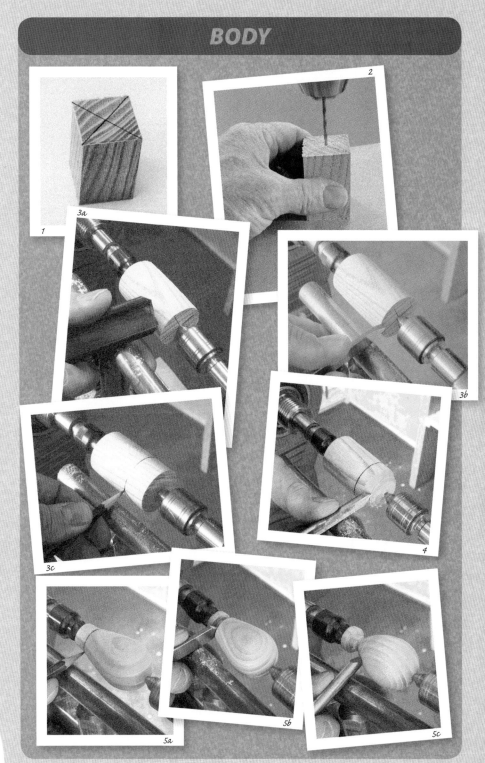

BODY

6 Start to form the rest of the profile with your spindle gouge (see the anatomy drawing). Make sure to form the side of the body with a gentle curve, again using a template if necessary. When the turning tool starts to get near the drive prongs, mark a pencil line around the blank at 2in (50mm) from the tailstock end **5a** . Use a thin parting tool to cut in a ¹³⁄₃₂in (10mm) spigot on the waste (headstock) side **5b** . Continue with the spindle gouge to form the profile. Don't reduce the drive spigot to less than ⁵⁄₁₆in (8mm) diameter at this stage. The turning should resemble a pointed egg shape **5c** .

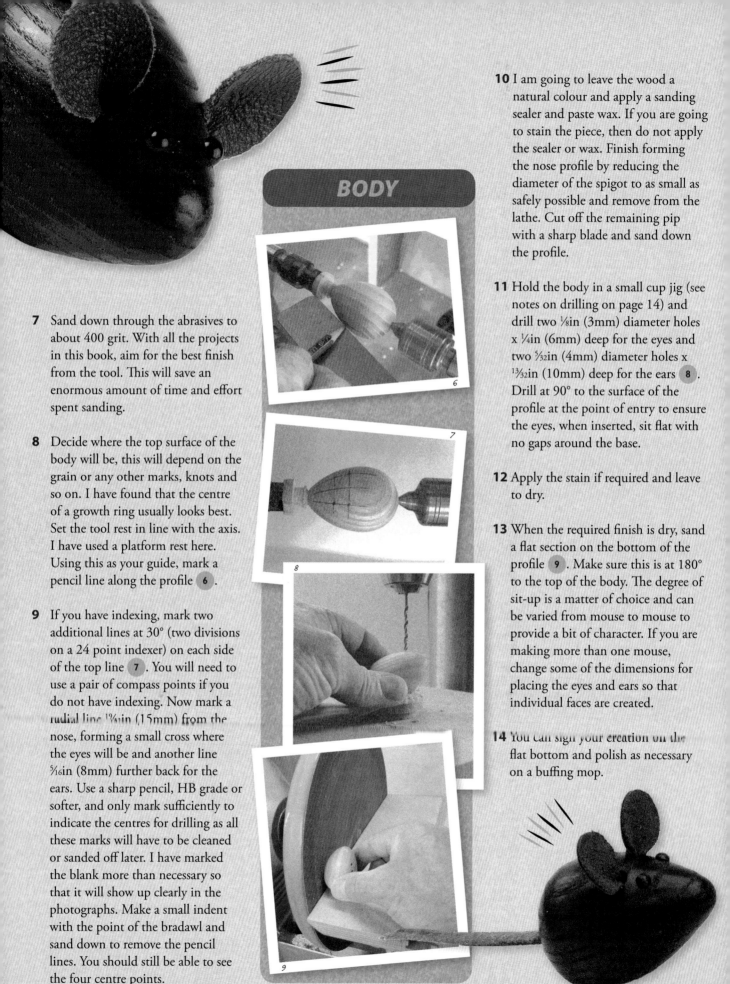

10 I am going to leave the wood a natural colour and apply a sanding sealer and paste wax. If you are going to stain the piece, then do not apply the sealer or wax. Finish forming the nose profile by reducing the diameter of the spigot to as small as safely possible and remove from the lathe. Cut off the remaining pip with a sharp blade and sand down the profile.

11 Hold the body in a small cup jig (see notes on drilling on page 14) and drill two ⅛in (3mm) diameter holes x ¼in (6mm) deep for the eyes and two ⁵⁄₃₂in (4mm) diameter holes x ¹³⁄₃₂in (10mm) deep for the ears ❽. Drill at 90° to the surface of the profile at the point of entry to ensure the eyes, when inserted, sit flat with no gaps around the base.

12 Apply the stain if required and leave to dry.

13 When the required finish is dry, sand a flat section on the bottom of the profile ❾. Make sure this is at 180° to the top of the body. The degree of sit-up is a matter of choice and can be varied from mouse to mouse to provide a bit of character. If you are making more than one mouse, change some of the dimensions for placing the eyes and ears so that individual faces are created.

14 You can sign your creation on the flat bottom and polish as necessary on a buffing mop.

BODY

7 Sand down through the abrasives to about 400 grit. With all the projects in this book, aim for the best finish from the tool. This will save an enormous amount of time and effort spent sanding.

8 Decide where the top surface of the body will be, this will depend on the grain or any other marks, knots and so on. I have found that the centre of a growth ring usually looks best. Set the tool rest in line with the axis. I have used a platform rest here. Using this as your guide, mark a pencil line along the profile ❻.

9 If you have indexing, mark two additional lines at 30° (two divisions on a 24 point indexer) on each side of the top line ❼. You will need to use a pair of compass points if you do not have indexing. Now mark a radial line ¹⁹⁄₃₂in (15mm) from the nose, forming a small cross where the eyes will be and another line ⁵⁄₁₆in (8mm) further back for the ears. Use a sharp pencil, HB grade or softer, and only mark sufficiently to indicate the centres for drilling as all these marks will have to be cleaned or sanded off later. I have marked the blank more than necessary so that it will show up clearly in the photographs. Make a small indent with the point of the bradawl and sand down to remove the pencil lines. You should still be able to see the four centre points.

EYES

1 Turn a length of dark wood down to a diameter of ⁵⁄₃₂in (4mm) **1a**, radius the end and form a spigot of ⅛in (3mm) diameter x ³⁄₁₆in (5mm) long (see anatomy drawing) **1b**.

EARS

The ears are cut from thin leather. Follow the pattern shown on the anatomy drawing.

TAIL

The tail is made from a 2⁹⁄₁₆in (65mm) length of leather shoelace and is slightly tapered at the end.

ASSEMBLY

1 The picture **2** shows the parts ready for assembly. Glue in the eyes. Do not rely on a tight push in fit as they may become loose as the wood dries further.

2 Glue in the ears and the tail.

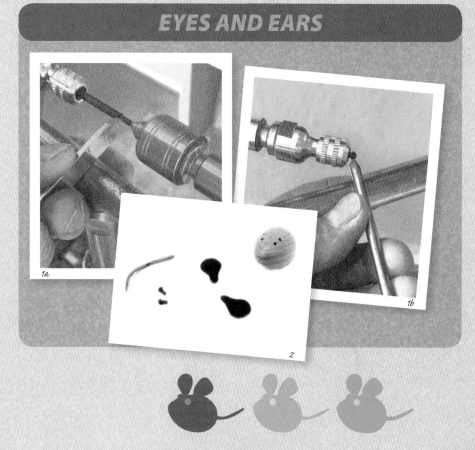

EYES AND EARS

1a

1b

2

VARIATIONS

As shown in the photograph, the variations are not only in colour, but in the huge variety of timbers you can choose from. We have a box of smaller ones in different colours to use for the counters in board games.

You may be surprised to discover how popular these toys are with children. Scale the basic shape up or down to create whole families of mice, your children's imagination will do the rest!

It would be hard to imagine a toy book without a chapter or two about spinning tops. There are literally hundreds of different shapes, sizes and designs of tops and no doubt you will probably have made one at some time. You will almost certainly have been given a top of some description as a child and have spent many happy hours playing with it.

The top I have chosen for this project not only spins, but also performs a second function. By fitting a pencil, crayon, felt tip or gel pen, the top will create intricate and colourful patterns according to the pen used.

PENCIL TOPS

It is compelling watching the patterns appear as the top spins its way across the page. There is almost no limit to the number of different shapes and styles that can be used, in addition to the huge range of pens and pencils that can be fitted in all colours.

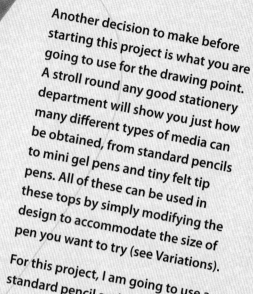

Another decision to make before starting this project is what you are going to use for the drawing point. A stroll round any good stationery department will show you just how many different types of media can be obtained, from standard pencils to mini gel pens and tiny felt tip pens. All of these can be used in these tops by simply modifying the design to accommodate the size of pen you want to try (see Variations).

For this project, I am going to use a standard pencil and leave the wood a natural colour with a finish of burnishing oil.

The main requirements for any top are a low centre of gravity and to be concentric; although with these tops the way the pencil is sharpened (a little off-centre for example) can result in some extraordinary patterns. When buying coloured pens, make sure the inks are non-toxic and safe for children. Watercolours are generally more suitable.

Cutting List

BODY
1 piece $2^{11}/_{32}$in x $2^{11}/_{32}$in x $1^{3}/_{16}$in (60mm x 60mm x 30mm) thick

FINIAL (optional)
1 piece $1^{9}/_{32}$in x $1^{9}/_{32}$in x $1^{9}/_{32}$in (15mm x 15mm x 15mm)
The finial makes the top easier to spin for small fingers.

In addition to the above you will need a standard pencil or crayon about 4in (100mm) long.

The choice of timber is yours and will depend on the type of finish you have in mind. I have chosen to use European olive (*Olea europaea*) for three reasons: it's hard and will withstand a few knocks in use, it's heavy with a specific gravity of 0.80, it will spin well giving a good definition to the pencil line. It's also a lovely timber, both to look at and to turn. Okay that's four.

ANATOMY DRAWING OF A PENCIL TOP

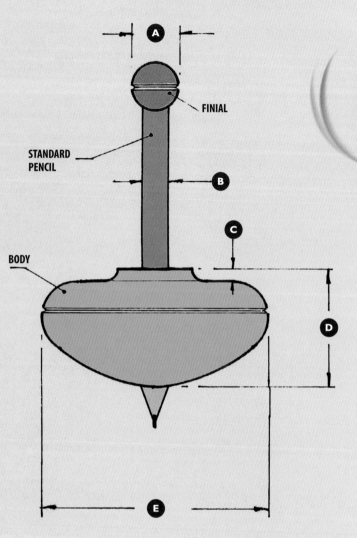

A

FINIAL

STANDARD PENCIL

B

C

BODY

D

E

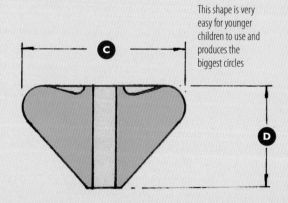

PENCIL TOPS

A $^{15}/_{32}$in (12mm) diameter

B $^{9}/_{32}$in (7mm) diameter approx

C $^{1}/_{8}$in (3mm)

D $1^{3}/_{16}$in (30mm)

E $2^{9}/_{32}$in (58mm) diameter

ALTERNATIVE SHAPES

A $2^{11}/_{32}$in (60mm) diameter

B $1^{3}/_{8}$in (35mm)

C $1^{31}/_{32}$in (50mm) diameter

D $1^{3}/_{16}$in (30mm)

ALTERNATIVE SHAPES

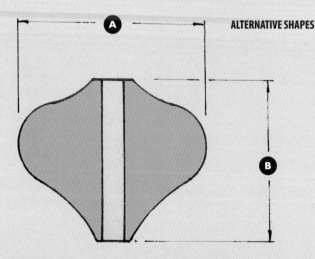

A

B

C

D

This shape is very easy for younger children to use and produces the biggest circles

BODY

1 Mark the diagonals on just one face of the blank and make a detent in the centre (**1**).

2 Scribe a 2¹¹⁄₃₂in (60mm) diameter circle around the centre point to act as a guide when cutting off the corners on the band saw.

3 Measure the diameter of the pencil. If it is hexagonal, measure across the corners and then drill a hole through the blank. The pencil needs to be a fairly tight fit, but not so tight that it is difficult to move. Try drilling a test piece first to check the fit. A smaller hole rather than one too large is preferable, as this can be eased with a file or sandpaper. If you do drill a hole too big, wrap some tape around the pencil to compensate (**2**). Cut off the corners.

4 Mount a piece of scrap timber into the jaws of a small chuck and turn a spigot to provide a tight fit in the hole you have just drilled. The spigot should be approximately ¹⁹⁄₃₂in (15mm) long (**3**).

5 This little jig will be used for mounting both the body and the finial (if used), so leave it in place until all the turning is completed.

6 Mount the body blank onto the spigot and bring up the tailstock centre for support. With a very sharp roughing gouge, turn the blank down to a cylinder, just removing any flat surfaces. A light touch and a sharp tool are needed (**4**).

BODY

1

2

3

4

7 Square up the ends and mark a line ²⁵⁄₃₂in (20mm) from the tailstock end **5a** . Form a radius or cone shape from the line down to the hole **5b** (see anatomy drawing).

8 Turn the top of the profile and make a decorative feature with a skew or three point tool around the waist (optional) **6a** . Sand as necessary and reverse the blank on the spigot to finish the top surface with the long point of a skew. Keep the left side of the bevel parallel with the surface being cut and arc the skew down toward the centre line **6b** .

9 Apply a coat of oil and leave it to soak for about 5–10 minutes. When the oil has lost its stickiness, burnish using a paper towel with the lathe running.

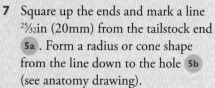

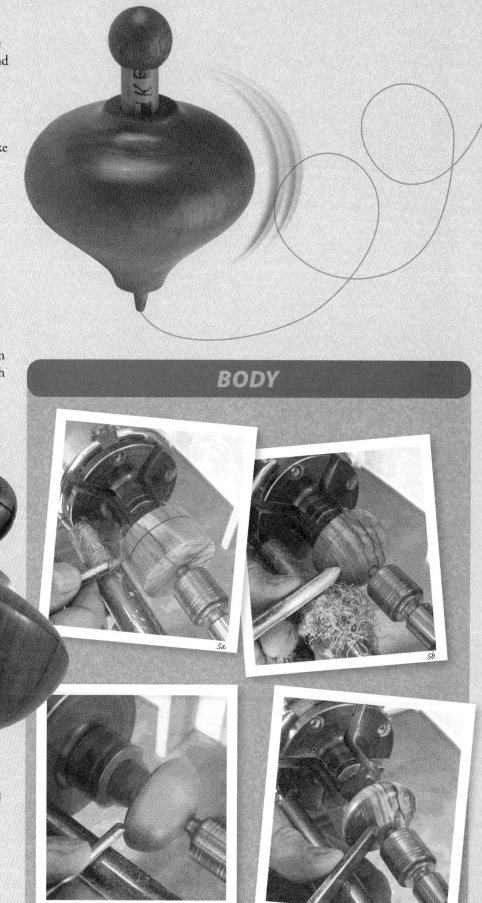

BODY

5a

5b

6a

6b

FINIAL

1 Mark the diagonals on one end of the cube and hold the piece in a drill table vice ①. Drill a hole the same size as drilled in the body blank x $^{13}\!/_{32}$in (10mm) deep. Mount the blank onto the spigot and bring up the tailstock for support. Turn down to a cylinder and square up the ends.

2 Mark a line in the centre ②a and, using a spindle gouge, form the radius ends ②b. Finish to match the body.

ASSEMBLY

1 Fit the pencil into the body, do not glue on the finial yet. Ease the diameter of the hole with a round file if necessary to allow the pencil to fit tightly but still be adjusted or removed as required.

TUNING

Try spinning the top by flicking the pencil between your thumb and middle finger onto a clean sheet of paper. The top should be just above the surface when released. Adjust the height of the top on the pencil to achieve different patterns. If the top will not spin or is top heavy, cut a short length off the end on the pencil and try again. Repeat this procedure until the top is well balanced. If you are using the finial, remove more of the pencil's length to compensate for the weight, then glue the finial in place.

FINIAL

VARIATIONS

An assortment of different shapes and styles can produce a wide variety of patterns, as shown in the photographs. You can also turn a hardwood spindle to replace the pencil and use it as an ordinary top.

KALEIDOSCOPIC COLOUR TOP

The Kaleidoscopic Colour Top consists of a string-operated top onto which is placed a coloured card disc, divided and sub-divided into blue, red, yellow and so on. When the top is spun it gives a kaleidoscope of colour. Pierced black discs add to the effect.

The timbers you choose for this project should be well-seasoned and stable. The centre axle has a hand chased screw thread so that it can be taken apart easily to fit in the little box I've made to keep all the bits together, but this is something you may decide for yourself. If you are not confident chasing threads, then you can just turn a spigot and glue the joint.

HISTORY

The Victorian home was very much the centre of family life. The period from about 1825 to 1900 saw the introduction of a great many optical discoveries. These adult novelties eventually became nursery toys. This top was introduced around 1860 as an optical learning device.

The high degree of craftsmanship demonstrated in making these devices is probably the main reason that so many now languish in museums and private collections. Surely no toy was made with that end in mind?

Cutting List

DISC PLATFORM

1 piece 5½in x 5½in x ¹⁹⁄₃₂in
(140mm x 140mm x 15mm) thick

HANDLE

1 piece 1⅜in x 1⅜in x 5²⁹⁄₃₂in
(34mm x 34mm x 150mm) long

STRING PULL

1 piece ¾in x ¾in x 2⅜in
(20mm x 20mm x 60mm) long

PIVOT POINT

1 piece 3¹⁄₃₂in x 3¹⁄₃₂in x 1³⁄₁₆in
(25mm x 25mm x 30mm) long

UPPER SPINDLE

1 piece 3¹⁄₃₂in x 3¹⁄₃₂in x 3¹⁵⁄₁₆in
(25mm x 25mm x 100mm) long

In addition, you will need a piece of string about 15in (40cm) long and paper or card for the coloured discs.

The wood I have chosen is pear (*Pyrus communis*) for the platform, handle and string pull, with Brazilian rosewood (*Dalbergia nigra*) for the centre spindle.

It is also a good idea to decide on the type of finish required as this can affect whether you need to work on or off the lathe to apply the various coatings. I am going to apply a sanding sealer to the pear, followed by paste wax, and then paste wax directly onto the rosewood. I will polish it on the lathe, so the warmth generated will let the wax soak in further. That's the theory anyway.

ANATOMY OF A
KALEIDOSCOPIC COLOUR TOP

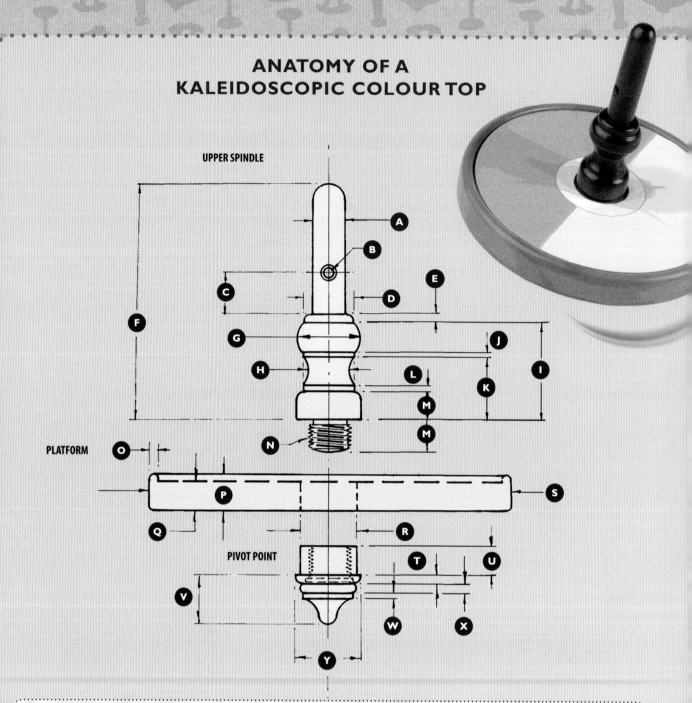

UPPER SPINDLE

PLATFORM

PIVOT POINT

UPPER SPINDLE

- **A** ¹⁵⁄₃₂in (12mm) diameter
- **B** ⅛in (3mm) diameter
- **C** ¹⁹⁄₃₂in (15mm)
- **D** ²³⁄₃₂in (18mm)
- **E** ³⁄₁₆in (5mm)
- **F** 3¹¹⁄₃₂in (85mm)
- **G** ²⁹⁄₃₂in (23mm) diameter
- **H** ¹⁹⁄₃₂in (15mm) diameter
- **I** 1¹¹⁄₃₂in (34mm)
- **J** ⁵⁄₆₄in (2mm)
- **K** ⅞in (22mm)
- **L** ⁵⁄₆₄in (2mm)
- **M** ¹³⁄₃₂in (10mm)
- **N** 20tpi x ¹⁹⁄₃₂in (15mm) diameter

PLATFORM

- **O** ⅛in (3mm)
- **P** ½in (13mm)
- **Q** ¹³⁄₃₂in (10mm)
- **R** ¾in (20mm) diameter
- **S** 5⅛in (130mm) diameter

PIVOT POINT

- **T** ⅛in (3mm)
- **U** ¹³⁄₃₂in (10mm)
- **V** ¹⁹⁄₃₂in (15mm)
- **W** ⁵⁄₆₄in (2mm)
- **X** ⅛in (3mm)
- **Y** ²⁹⁄₃₂in (23mm)

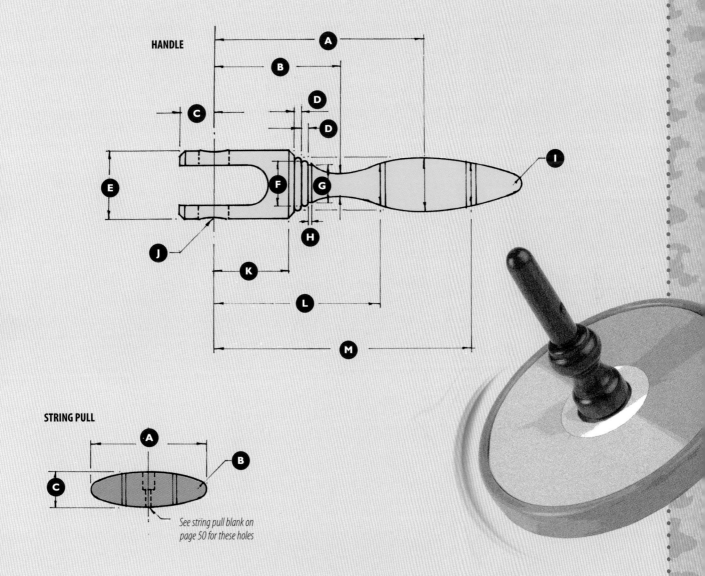

HANDLE

STRING PULL

See string pull blank on
page 50 for these holes

HANDLE

Ⓐ ²⁹⁄₃₂in (23mm) diameter at
3⅝in (92mm)

Ⓑ ¹⁵⁄₃₂in (12mm) at 2⁵⁄₃₂in (55mm)

Ⓒ ¹⁹⁄₃₂in (15mm)

Ⓓ ⅛in (3mm)

Ⓔ 1³⁄₁₆in (30mm) diameter

Ⓕ ²⁵⁄₃₂in (20mm)

Ⓖ ²³⁄₃₂in (18mm)

Ⓗ ⁵⁄₆₄in (2mm)

Ⓘ ³⁄₁₆in (5mm) radius

Ⓙ Centre line ⁹⁄₁₆in (14mm) diameter hole

Ⓚ 1⅜in (35mm)

Ⓛ ²¹⁄₃₂in (17mm) diameter at 2²⁷⁄₃₂in (72mm)

Ⓜ ²¹⁄₃₂in (17mm) diameter at 4¹³⁄₃₂in (112mm)

STRING PULL

Ⓐ 1³¹⁄₃₂in (50mm)

Ⓑ ⁵⁄₃₂in (4mm) radius

Ⓒ ¹⁹⁄₃₂in (15mm) diameter

UPPER SPINDLE

UPPER SPINDLE (stage 1)

1 Mark the diagonals on each end and mount between centres. Using a roughing gouge, reduce to a cylinder, just removing any flat surfaces. Square up the ends with a parting tool **1**.

2 Turn a ¹⁹⁄₃₂in (15mm) diameter x ¹⁵⁄₃₂in (12mm) long spigot at the tailstock end. Chamfer the end to give the chaser a start. Using a narrow parting tool, undercut the base of the spigot (see anatomy drawing) **2**.

3 Hand chase a right hand 20tpi (threads per inch), thread onto the spigot **3a**. Reduce the length of the thread to ¹³⁄₃₂in (10mm). Remove from the lathe and keep the blank in a safe place for finishing the profile later. The finished thread **3b**.

PLATFORM (stage 1)

1 Mark across the diagonals on one side of the blank and indent the centre with a bradawl. Scribe a 5⁵⁄₁₆in (135mm) diameter circle around this centre.

2 Cut out the circle on the band saw. This can be done freehand **1**.

3 Drill a ¾in (20mm) diameter hole through the centre of the blank **2**. Keep this blank safely to one side for finishing later.

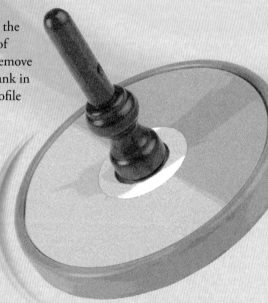

PLATFORM

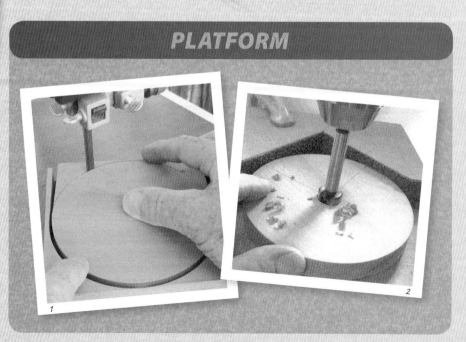

PIVOT POINT

1 Mark the diagonals at each end in the usual way and mount between centres. Turn down to a $^{29}/_{32}$in (23mm) diameter cylinder. Square up the ends.

2 Re-mount the blank in the compression jaws of a small chuck. This blank will now be used to mount the upper spindle and the platform so it's important to leave it in the chuck until these parts are finished. Leave $^{15}/_{32}$in (12mm) protruding from the chuck.

3 Accurately measure the root diameter (the diameter at the bottom of the thread) that you chased on the upper spindle **1**. Fit a Jacobs-type drill chuck in the tailstock quill and a saw tooth drill bit just smaller than the root diameter measured. The root on my thread measures $^{17}/_{32}$in (13½mm),

PIVOT POINT

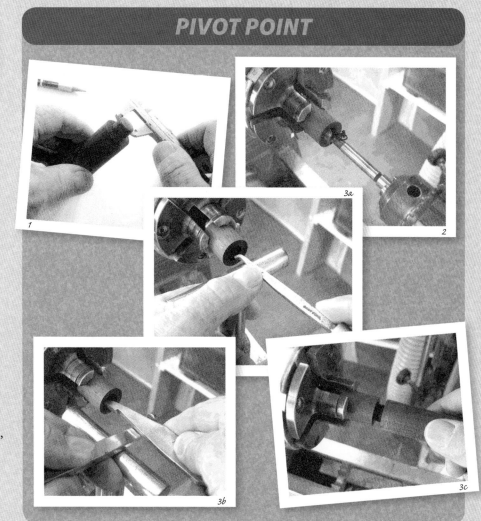

TOP TIP

If you prefer to use shavings from the turning to burnish or de-nib your work then it is vital not to mix different types of shaving together. As the harder timber, in this case rosewood, will scratch and possibly discolour the softer pear wood. Sweep up or vacuum the shavings after turning one timber to avoid contaminating the next batch.

so a ½in (12½mm) diameter drill will be used to drill a hole in the end of the pivot point blank x $^{15}/_{32}$in (12mm) deep. Keep the speed down to about 500rpm and progress slowly with the cut to minimize any heat checking **2**.

4 Cut a small recess at the bottom of the hole to give the chaser some clearance **3a**. Form a small chamfer at the mouth to start the thread and chase a matching thread to the one on the spindle **3b**. Keep trying the parts together until you achieve a good fit **3c**.

UPPER SPINDLE (stage 2)

1 Screw in the upper spindle and bring up the tailstock for support. Use a parting tool and a pencil to mark out the positions and diameters of the profile **1** .

2 With all the relevant dimensions blocked in, you can form the profile using a small spindle gouge **2a** . Sand down through the grits as necessary to 400 or 600 grit and apply some paste wax with the lathe running. Leave for a few minutes and then buff to a shine with a paper towel **2b** .

3 Unscrew the spindle, leaving the pivot in the chuck. Cut off the waste pip at the end of the spindle and sand and polish the profile. Drill a ⅛in (3mm) diameter hole through the spindle (see anatomy drawing).

Chamfer the edges of the hole so it is easier to thread the string **3a** .

The next job is to finish turning the platform. With the pivot point still in the chuck, turn down the outside diameter to suit the ¾in (20mm) hole drilled in the platform x $^{13}/_{32}$in (10mm) long. Ensure the platform is a push fit onto the pivot and sits squarely. Rotate the lathe by hand to check that it is running fairly concentrically. When you are satisfied with the fit, glue in place and leave until the adhesive has cured, preferably overnight **3b** .

Note: If you need to remove the assembly from the lathe, leave it mounted in the chuck and remove the chuck/pivot and platform as one.

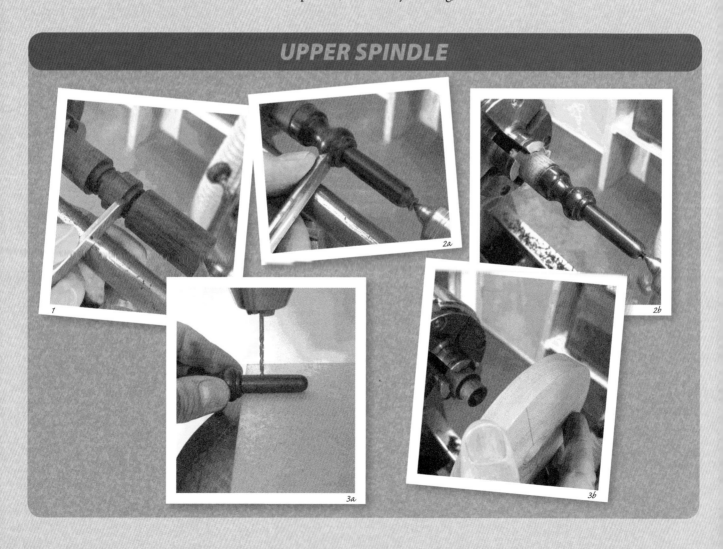

UPPER SPINDLE

1

2a

2b

3a

3b

PLATFORM

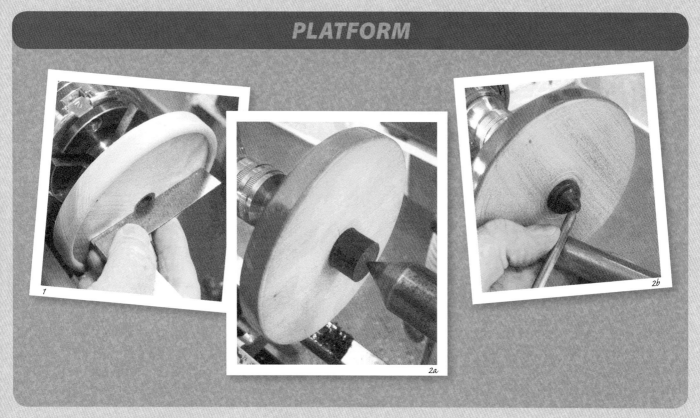

PLATFORM (stage 2)

1 When the glue has dried, use a small gouge to trim the outer edge of the disc and to cut a recess in the face of the platform down to the pivot point. Do not remove any material from the pivot point as this may affect the fit of the spindle. Keep an eye on the face of the platform to ensure it is flat **1** . Work carefully and gently here, finishing with a shearing cut or freshly sharpened scraper. Pear wood cuts beautifully and you should get a very good finish with the tool. Sand down to 400 grit and apply sanding sealer. When this is dry, de-nib with fine Webrax or shavings from the pear.

2 Apply some paste wax and allow to dry before buffing to a fine finish. Screw on the upper spindle and check that everything runs true.

3 Reverse mount the assembly using the ¹⁵⁄₃₂in (12mm) shaft of the upper spindle. Use soft jaws if you have them or protect the finish using tape **2a** . Bring up the tailstock for support and gently true up the rear face of the platform. Sand, seal and finish to match the other side, then turn the profile of the pivot point. Apply some wax to this area and buff **2b** .

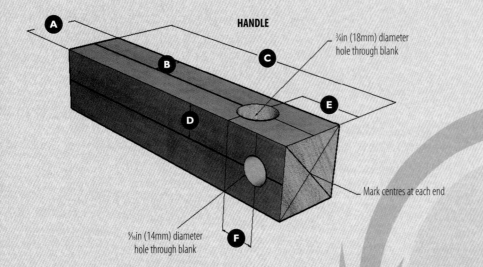

HANDLE

¾in (18mm) diameter
hole through blank

Mark centres at each end

⁹⁄₁₆in (14mm) diameter
hole through blank

HANDLE BLANK

A 1³⁄₈in (34mm) square

B ¹¹⁄₁₆in (17mm)

C 5²⁹⁄₃₂in (150mm)

D ¹¹⁄₁₆in (17mm)

E 1³⁄₁₆in (30mm)

F ¹⁹⁄₃₂in (15mm)

HANDLE

1 Mark the diagonals on the ends of the blank and the centre points with a bradawl. Also mark the centres of the two holes as shown in the drawing above.

2 Drill a ¾in (18mm) diameter hole through the blank. Use a backing board to minimize breakout **1a** . Drill another hole at 90° to the first. This one is ⁹⁄₁₆in (14mm) diameter and also goes through the blank **1b** .

3 Mount the blank between centres with the two holes nearer the headstock end. Turn down to a 1³⁄₁₆in (30mm) diameter cylinder **2a** . Mark a pencil line 1³¹⁄₃₂in (50mm) from the headstock end

and reduce the diameter to ²⁹⁄₃₂in (23mm) from this line to the tailstock end **2b** . Square up both ends and form a chamfer at the headstock end.

4 Mark and cut the relevant points along the handle **3a** . Then using a small spindle gouge, form the profile. Leave a safe working diameter as a spigot for the tailstock and add some decorative rings with a skew or three-point tool **3b** .

5 Sand the profile down to 400 grit, seal and finish. Remove from the lathe and cut off the pip at the end. Sand in to match the profile, then seal and polish the end.

6 You can cut the slot by hand, but the simple handle cutting jig makes a more professional job and is safer **4** . Use a fine blade and finish sanding the inside faces by hand. Seal and polish to match the rest of the handle.

HANDLE CUTTING JIG

A 2in (50mm)

B ¹¹⁄₁₆in (17mm)

C 5³⁄₈in (135mm)

D 1in (25mm)

E 1³⁄₈in (34mm)

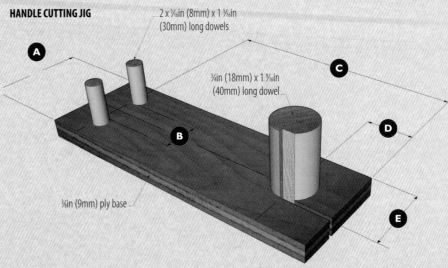

2 x ⁵⁄₁₆in (8mm) x 1³⁄₁₆in (30mm) long dowels

¾in (18mm) x 1⁹⁄₁₆in (40mm) long dowel

⅜in (9mm) ply base

HANDLE

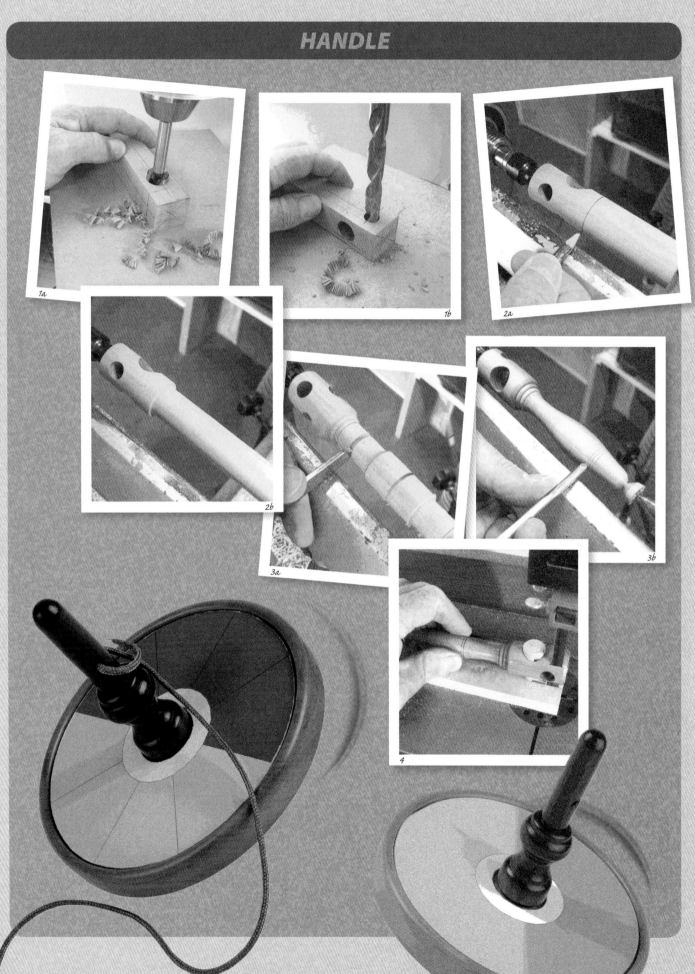

1a

1b

2a

2b

3a

3b

4

STRING PULL

1 Mark the centres at each end of the blank. Mark the blank in accordance with the drawing below and drill a ³⁄₁₆in (5mm) diameter hole x ³⁄₈in (10mm) deep in one side. Drill a ⁵⁄₆₄in (2mm) diameter hole through to the other side **1**.

2 Mount between centres and reduce down to a ¹⁹⁄₃₂in (15mm) diameter cylinder. Mark a line around the centre, where the hole is, then mark two lines equidistant from the centre using a compass point **2**.

3 Turn the profile. If you are not happy turning close to the prongs of the drive centre, then just reverse mount the blank to turn each end at the tailstock **3**. Cut in any decoration required before sanding, sealing and polishing to match the handle. Reduce the ends to as small as safely possible before removing from the lathe.

4 Cut off the end pips with a sharp knife and sand the end profile. Seal and wax to complete the turning.

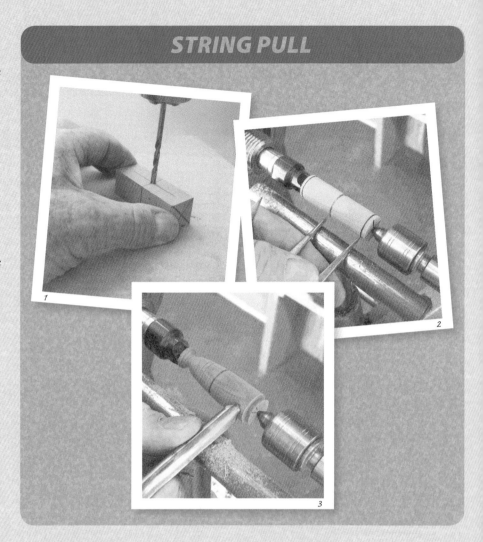

STRING PULL

Drill ³⁄₁₆in (5mm) diameter x ³⁄₈in (10mm) deep, then ⁵⁄₆₄in (2mm) diameter through on the same centre

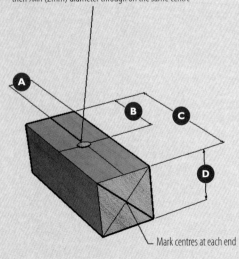

Mark centres at each end

STRING PULL BLANK

A ³⁄₈in (10mm)

B 1³⁄₁₆in (30mm)

C 2³⁄₈in (60mm)

D ³⁄₄in (20mm) square

PAPER OR CARD COLOUR DISCS

1 Make some circular paper or card discs to fit inside the rim of your platform. The hole in the centre should be just large enough to fit over the spindle and lie flat on the platform.

ASSEMBLY

With all the parts turned and polished, the assembly is very straightforward. Screw the upper spindle into position, place a disc on the platform and fit the handle onto the spindle.

Tie a knot in one end of the string and thread the other end through the large hole in the string pull and out through the small hole. Pull the knot into the larger hole. Thread the string through the hole in the upper spindle with about ½–⅝in (10–15mm) protruding. Then wind the top to wrap the string around the spindle. Holding the handle in one hand and the string pull in the other, and with the platform and pivot just above the surface you want it to spin on, pull the string off the spindle causing the top to spin and drop away from the handle.

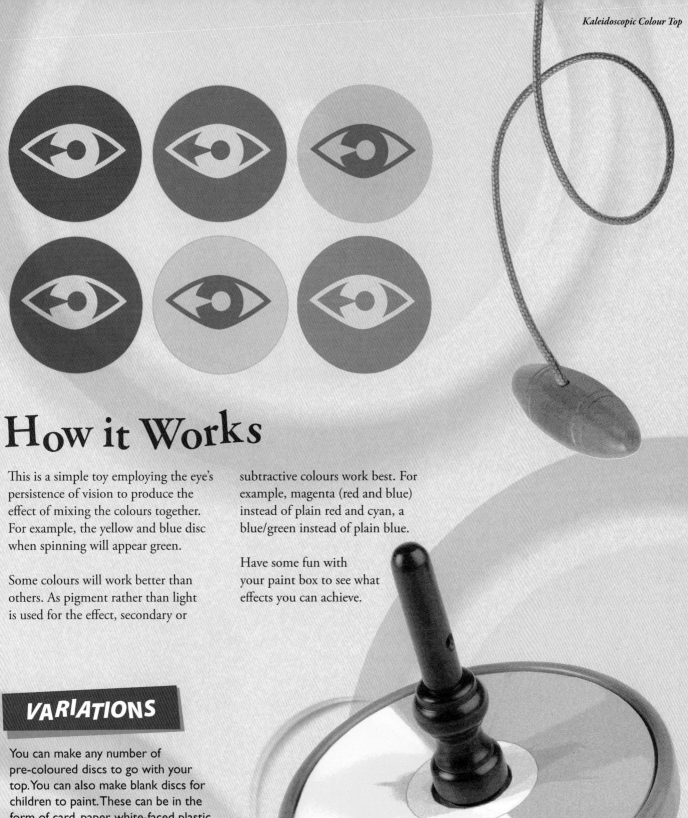

How it Works

This is a simple toy employing the eye's persistence of vision to produce the effect of mixing the colours together. For example, the yellow and blue disc when spinning will appear green.

Some colours will work better than others. As pigment rather than light is used for the effect, secondary or subtractive colours work best. For example, magenta (red and blue) instead of plain red and cyan, a blue/green instead of plain blue.

Have some fun with your paint box to see what effects you can achieve.

VARIATIONS

You can make any number of pre-coloured discs to go with your top. You can also make blank discs for children to paint. These can be in the form of card, paper, white-faced plastic or hardboard. Whiteboard markers are another medium that can be used, making the discs re-usable. Patterns in the form of rings or black perforated cards can all add to the many effects. Seeing who can produce the most colourful or surprising effect is a great way to keep the children amused on a rainy day.

STACKING DISCS

This toy is ideal for promoting hand and eye co-ordination, as well as colour and shape recognition for the very young child. Initially the play will involve just placing the discs onto the spindle, but this will soon develop into getting the sizes or colours in a recognized order. There are also no small parts or sharp edges and the colours chosen are very bright and cheerful.

I am using
European ash
(Fraxinus excelsior)
for the discs, the base
and the spindle, as well as
the ball on the top. Of course,
you can use any timber you
prefer. If you have the benefit
of a planer or thicknesser and can
prepare a plank beforehand, then you
will save an appreciable amount of time.

Cutting List

BASE
1 piece 5½in x 5½in x 31/32in
(140mm x 140mm x 25mm) thick

DISC 1
1 piece 4¹⁵/₁₆in x 4¹⁵/₁₆in x 31/32in
(125mm x 125mm x 25mm) thick

DISC 2
1 piece 4¹¹/₃₂in x 4¹¹/₃₂in x 31/32in
(110mm x 110mm x 25mm) thick

DISC 3
1 piece 3¾in x 3¾in x 31/32in
(95mm x 95mm x 25mm) thick

DISC 4
1 piece 3¹¹/₃₂in x 3¹¹/₃₂in x 31/32in
(85mm x 85mm x 25mm) thick

DISC 5
1 piece 2¾in x 2¾in x 31/32in
(70mm x 70mm x 25mm) thick

DISC 6
1 piece 2⁵/₃₂in x 2⁵/₃₂in x 31/32in
(55mm x 55mm x 25mm) thick

BALL
1 piece 1³¹/₃₂in x 1³¹/₃₂in x 1³¹/₃₂in
(50mm x 50mm x 50mm)

SPINDLE
1 piece 29/32in x 29/32in x 7in
(23mm x 23mm x 180mm) long

The cutting list, as usual, gives dimensions in the square, but you may determine the sizes needed from your own stock availability. I have allowed the grain to show through in the finished article however, if you are going to paint the discs with an opaque finish then you can use different or less expensive timbers for each disc.

The turning itself is really very basic, all the discs are cut, drilled and turned in an identical manner. I have found the expanding spigot chuck a real bonus and well worth the time taken to make it. See the drawing on page 56 for details.

For the finish, I have used a thin stain (various colours) followed by several coats of a toy safe melamine lacquer, all applied off the lathe.

ANATOMY DRAWING OF STACKING DISCS

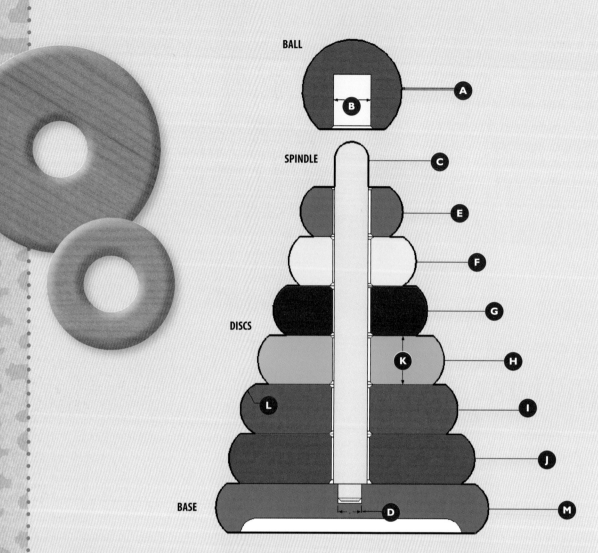

BALL

SPINDLE

DISCS

BASE

BALL

A 1¹³⁄₁₆in (46mm)

B ¾in (20mm) diameter

SPINDLE

C ¹¹⁄₁₆in (18mm) diameter

D ¹⁹⁄₃₂in (15mm)diameter
x ¹¹⁄₃₂in (9mm) long spigot

DISCS

E 1³¹⁄₃₂in (50mm) diameter

F 2⁹⁄₁₆in (65mm) diameter

G 3⁵⁄₃₂in (80mm) diameter

H 3¹⁷⁄₃₂in (90mm) diameter

I 4⅛in (105mm) diameter

J 4²³⁄₃₂in (120mm) diameter

K ²⁹⁄₃₂in (23mm)

L 1³⁄₁₆in (21mm) radius

BASE

M 5⁵⁄₁₆in (135mm) diameter

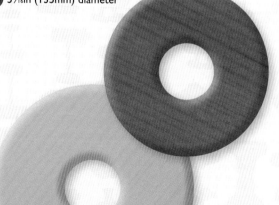

BASE

1 Mark across the corners of the 5½in (140mm) square blank to find the centre and scribe a circle in pencil to use as a guide when cutting out the shape on the band saw.

2 Drill a hole in the centre of the blank to suit a screw chuck x ¹³⁄₃₂in (10mm) deep and cut the blank into a 5½in (140mm) approximate diameter disc.

3 Mount the blank onto the screw chuck and cut a dovetail recess to suit your own expansion chuck **1a**. Use a straight edge to ensure the base is flat **1b**.

4 Reverse mount the blank onto an expansion chuck and square up the front face leaving an overall thickness of ²⁹⁄₃₂in (23mm).

5 Use a small bowl gouge, or whatever you prefer, to turn the outside profile of the base. Use a template if necessary to get all the discs the same shape **2**.

6 Enlarge the centre hole to ¹⁹⁄₃₂in (15mm) diameter x ¹³⁄₃₂in (10mm) deep **3**.

7 Sand down through the grits as necessary to 400 grit abrasive.

8 Remove from the lathe and remount onto a ¹⁹⁄₃₂in (15mm) diameter spigot or a set of cole jaws if you have some. Use a blanking piece over the tailstock to prevent marking the base and finish the underside, softening the dovetail with a radius. Hand sand the bottom of the base and remove from the lathe **4**.

BASE

1a

1b

2

3

4

SPINDLE

1 Mark the diagonals on each end of the blank and mount between centres ❶ . Rough down to a cylinder, just removing any flat surfaces.

2 Use a skew chisel to plane the surface down to a diameter of $^{11}/_{16}$in (18mm). Radius the end at the tailstock leaving enough waste diameter to hold the blank for sanding ❷ .

3 Measure the length required; this will be six disc thicknesses, plus the ball recess and a further $^{11}/_{32}$in (9mm) for the spigot fixing in the base. In the example here, I need a 6⅝in (170mm) overall length.

4 Reduce the diameter at the headstock end to suit the spigot hole in the base x $^{11}/_{32}$in (9mm) long ❸ . Form a small chamfer on the end to ease assembly.

5 Sand the surface down through the grits as necessary and then reduce the waste at each end to as small as safely possible then remove from the lathe. Cut off the waste and sand in the profile on top.

EXPANDING SPIGOT CHUCK

All the discs are made in a similar manner and are mounted on the lathe using the expanding spigot chuck detailed below. The chuck is very simple to turn and will more than repay the time that it takes to make. Almost any timber can be used. I have chosen Idigbo (*Terminalia ivorensis*) for the main body of the chuck. This is normally straight grained but fairly coarse and the texture is moderately open. It is not generally considered as one of the mainstream woodturning timbers and is therefore relatively inexpensive when purchased in large pieces from carpentry outlets. I always try to keep some on my stock shelves as the texture makes excellent jam chucks, glue chucks and spigot or mandrel chucks. For the plug I have used European beech (*Fagus sylvatic*).

SPINDLE

1

2

3

EXPANDING SPIGOT CHUCK

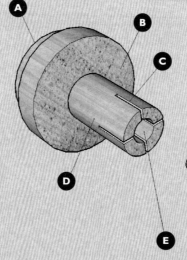

A

B

C

D

E

F

G

EXPANDING SPIGOT CHUCK

A Dovetail to suit your own chuck

B 1$^{31}/_{32}$in (50mm) diameter x $^{13}/_{32}$in (10mm) approx

C 4 x saw cuts at 90 spacing x ¾in (20mm) long

D ¾in (20mm) diameter x 1⅜in (35mm) long spigot

E ⅜in (10mm) diameter hole drilled through centre of chuck to allow knocking out of plug if necessary

F $^{31}/_{32}$in (25mm) long plug tapering $^{11}/_{32}$in (9mm) diameter to ½in (12mm) diameter

G Tailstock centre

DISCS

DISCS

1. Mark across the diagonals on one face of the blank and scribe the maximum diameter possible on each blank using a pencil compass.

2. Drill a ¾in (20mm) diameter hole through the centre of each blank. Cut the blanks into discs on the band saw using the pencil lines as a guide **1**.

3. Mount the spigot chuck in your own compression chuck **2a**. Fit the first disc on the spigot chuck and insert the plug. Bring up the tailstock into the centre mark of the plug **2b**.

4. Use a straight edge to determine the flatness of the face and square up the face as necessary **3a**. I am using a sharp scraper here as this works for me. Try to get shavings, even with a scraper, as this will produce a finer finish **3b**. Sand the face as required down to 400 grit.

5. Withdraw the tailstock point if it's used. Then ease out the plug to allow the disc to slide over the end of the chuck sufficiently to form a 5⁄64in (2mm) chamfer around the hole. This will help the child to locate the spindle when it's in use **4**.

6. Reverse mount the disc and repeat step 4 to refine the other face. This will also thickness the discs which should all be the same.

7. Use a small bowl gouge to form the outside profile at the diameter required for the particular disc being turned. Use the template if necessary to keep the profiles consistent.

8. Sand the face and edge profile. Then form the chamfer on this side before removing from the lathe. Make another five discs using exactly the same method.

BALL

1 Mark the diagonals on one of the end grain faces of the $1^{31}/_{32}$in (50mm) cube and drill a ¾in (20mm) diameter hole x $1^{3}/_{16}$in (30mm) deep in the centre.

2 Mount the blank on the spigot chuck (without the plug) and bring up the tailstock point. If the chuck is a little loose, you can simply make a plug to fit inside and expand the chuck slightly (see Top Tip).

3 Turn the cube down to a $1^{7}/_{8}$in (48mm) diameter cylinder and mark a line around the centre. You may wish to use the sphere turning jig shown on page 21. Follow the guidance given to turn the ball. If you are turning the ball by hand, use a spindle gouge and work from the main diameter down to the centre, removing equal amounts each pass to form the perfect sphere **1**.

4 Use a point tool or similar to form a chamfer around the hole. This may cut into the wooden chuck, but it does not matter as you have now finished with it.

5 Sand the sphere by hand as necessary and remove from the lathe.

All the parts are now turned and ready for applying the finish **2**.

BALL

VARIATIONS

The choice of colours and finish can make a tremendous difference to the appearance and use of this toy. There is also no reason to limit the toy to simple discs. The same assembled format can be made to resemble simple animal or human shapes (see the Stacking Figure on page 120). Of course, you can use different timbers if you really do not like painting or staining wood.

TOP TIP

Be careful here as too much pressure from the tailstock could force the plug into the chuck, and make the ball too tight or impossible to remove.

In this event, you can drift out the plug through the hollow headstock spindle if available. Or at worst, remove the whole chuck and insert a drift from the back.

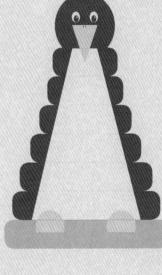

YO-YO

The simplest toys have been in existence for thousands of years and have remained basically the same. The Return Top was known to the ancient Greek and Egyptian civilizations of 3,500 years ago and examples have been found from pre-Christian China. The term *joujou* (the French word for toy) was applied to a toy of this type by M. Preller, a French archaeologist, in 1852 when ceramic discs were found dating back to about 500BC.

The toy does not appear to have been known in Europe before the eighteenth century when it was introduced as the *emigrette*. It is one of those toys that sweeps over Europe and America as a craze in every generation. One of the first such crazes was recorded back in 1789–90, when the toy was more popularly known as a *bandilor* in France and as a *quiz* in England.

Several toy companies built their fortunes on the manufacture of these Return Tops, as the Chinese called them, including the Yo-Yo Company whose name probably popularized the now generic name; also Louis Marx's company the Girard Model Works in Pennsylvania, which re-introduced the yo-yo in 1928 and sold them in their millions.

Cutting List

BODY

2 pieces 2⁹⁄₁₆in x 2⁹⁄₁₆in x ²³⁄₃₂in
(65mm x 65mm x 18mm) thick

DISCS

1 piece 1⅜in x 1⅜in x 1³⁄₁₆in
(35mm x 35mm x 30mm) long

AXLE

1 piece ¹⁵⁄₃₂in x ¹⁵⁄₃₂in x 1⅜in
(12mm x 12mm x 35mm) long

In addition to the above you will need a piece of string about 40in (1m) long.

My version of the toy is made using two contrasting timbers. The main body shows side grain and a central end grain disc with some decorative chatter work. I have chosen European cherry (*Prunus avium*) for the body and purpleheart (*Peltogyne spp*) for the discs. The finish is a cellulose sanding sealer with a melamine lacquer on top.

ANATOMY DRAWING OF A YO-YO

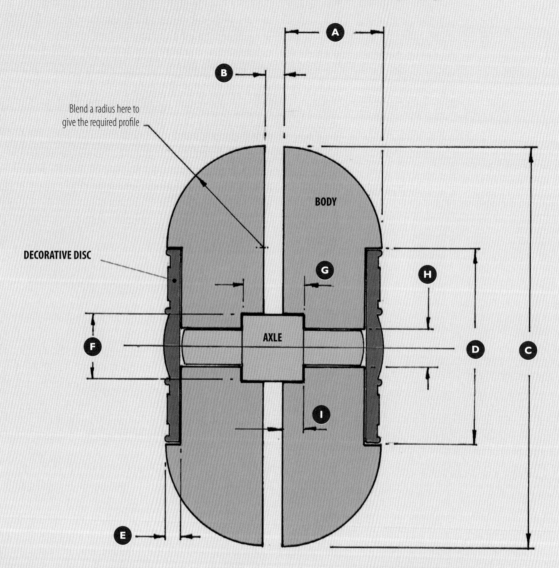

Blend a radius here to give the required profile

DECORATIVE DISC

BODY

AXLE

BODY

A ⅝in (16mm)

B ⅛in (3mm)

C 2¹¹⁄₃₂in (60mm) diameter

DISCS

D 1³⁄₁₆in (30mm) diameter

E ⅛in (3mm)

AXLE

F ¹³⁄₃₂in (10mm) diameter

G ⅜in (9mm)

H ¼in (6mm)

I ⅛in (3mm)

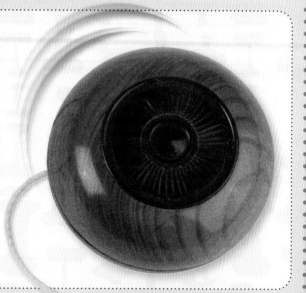

BODY

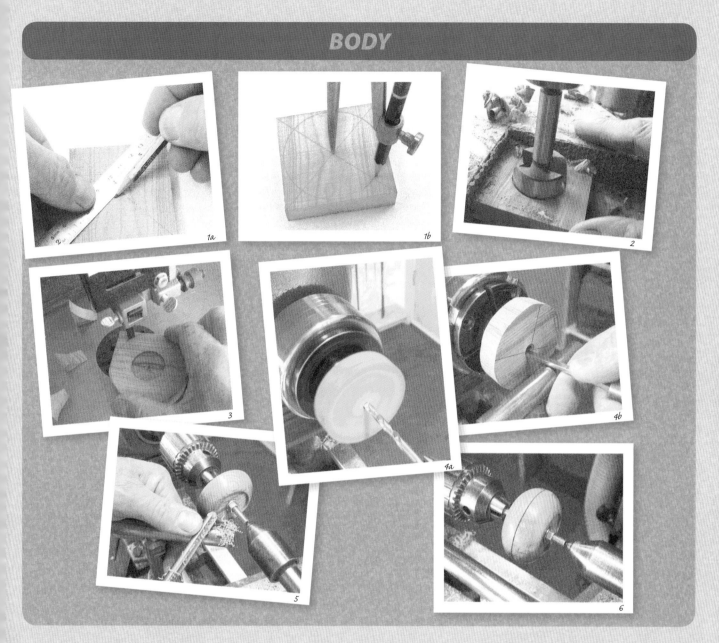

BODY

1 Mark the diagonals on the face of the blank **1a** . Scribe a circle of 2⅞₆in (62mm) diameter in pencil to give a guide to cutting out the body on the band saw **1b** .

2 Drill a 1³⁄₁₆in (30mm) diameter hole (or a size to suit your own small expansion chuck) x ³⁄₁₆in (5mm) deep in the centre of one face **2** .

3 Cut the blank on the band saw around the pencil line **3** .

4 Mount the blank on a small expansion chuck and square up the face as necessary. Drill a ¼in (6mm) diameter hole through the blank **4a** and, using a small scraper, turn a recess ¹³⁄₃₂in (10mm) diameter x ⅛in (3mm) deep around the ¼in (6mm) hole **4b** (see the anatomy drawing). Sand and seal the face.

5 Re-mount the blank onto a ¼in (6mm) mandrel with the large recess now facing the tailstock and turn the outside profile **5** . Repeat steps 1–5 for the other half of the body.

6 Mount both halves of the body **6** and refine the shape as necessary. Sand down to 400 grit and apply a coat of cellulose sealer. As a precaution to prevent the halves sticking together, fit a washer onto the mandrel between the halves before sealing.

7 Apply two or three coats of melamine, flatting down between coats and leave to dry.

DECORATIVE DISCS

1 Mount the blank directly into the compression jaws of your chuck with the grain parallel to the bed. Turn down to a diameter of 1³⁄₁₆in (30mm) or to suit your own recess dimension.

2 Use a narrow parting tool or small gouge to define the areas where you are going to add decoration **1**.

3 Set the lathe speed to give the chosen effect. In this example the speed is 1500rpm **2a**. When you have created your pattern, clean it up with a small point tool as necessary **2b** and seal with the cellulose sanding sealer. Finish with a coat of melamine.

4 Measure the actual depth of the recess in the body then part off the disc to suit **3**.

5 Make another disc from the remaining blank.

AXLE

1 Turn the axle according to the dimensions shown in the anatomy drawing. I am using a piece of beech, but any scrap or off cut will do. The finished length will be 1¹⁄₁₆in (28mm) to ensure the axle does not interfere with the fitting of the decorative discs later.

ASSEMBLY

1 Dry fit all the parts together to ensure all is well and that you have a ⅛in (3mm) equal gap all round. Adjust the fit if necessary before gluing all the parts together.

2 Tie the string around the hub and wind it onto the axle. You are now ready to get practising or make some more, ready for the next craze.

FITTING A BEARING TO THE AXLE

To turbo-charge your yo-yo the following materials will be required:

1x ball bearing

1x 1¹⁄₁₆in (28mm) long dowel

Measure the dimensions of your chosen bearing. An inner diameter of ¼in (6mm) would be ideal and will fit straight onto a standard dowel.

Refer to step 4 on page 63 (turning the body) and cut a recess as detailed to suit your own bearing.

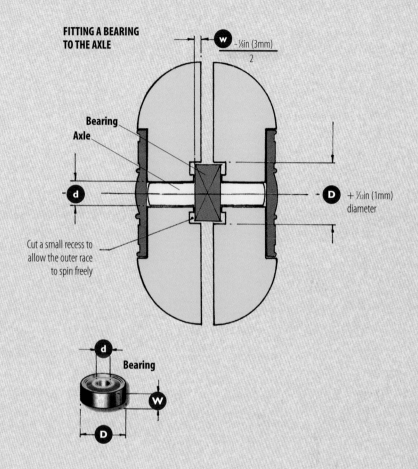

FITTING A BEARING TO THE AXLE

w − ⅛in (3mm) / 2

Bearing

Axle

d

D + ¹⁄₂in (1mm) diameter

Cut a small recess to allow the outer race to spin freely

d

Bearing

W

D

VARIATIONS

The basic yo-yo design has not changed much for more than 3,000 years, but new materials have brought about improvements to the action. There are two significant changes you can make to improve the way the toy performs.

STRING

Any knots or obstructions in the string will create resistance to the spin and slow the toy down, as will tying the line too tightly to the axle. You can make a simple twisted loop in some cotton twine. Better still, you can purchase specially woven replacement yo-yo strings from good toy shops. These are simply looped over the body onto the axle, giving a knot free line.

AXLE

The most significant improvement you can make is to replace the axle with a dowel onto which a ball bearing is fitted, see anatomy drawing. A ¼in (6mm) bearing is a fairly standard size for router bits, and is therefore readily available from tool stores. The width and outside diameter will vary slightly between manufacturers, so it makes sense to obtain the bearing first and then follow the guidance in the drawing above. There are many variations you can make to the appearance of the toy as shown on page 7.

How it Works

The yo-yo depends on its rotary motion and inertia to rewind on the cord. Take several turns of the string around the axle, hold onto the free end and drop or throw the top towards the ground. As the string unwinds, the top spins about its axis. The faster it rotates, the more stable it becomes.

The top will only fall to the extent of the string. At this point, the player can impart a slight jerk upwards (this is where the practice comes in). The kinetic energy is converted to inertia and as the top continues to spin it appears to climb back up, rewinding the string around the axle as it goes. It will not return all the way. Friction of the cord on the sides and wind resistance will cause the top to lose energy. The player must now lower his hand to meet the returning top and rewind the string completely. At this point, a quick upward movement of the hand starts the string unwinding, but because of inertia the whole top is lifted. The top then starts to fall again and the action is repeated. With a lot of practice the toy can do some amazing tricks.

SKITTLES

The version of the game made in this project uses wooden balls rather than the 'cheese'.

The timber used can be the same for all nine pins and the wooden balls.

It can be laminated or cut from the solid hardwood or softwood and the whole set can be sized to suit your own conditions.

The preparation and turning is very basic and gives an opportunity for repetition turning.

Nine identically sized pins will be required, together with two or three perfect spheres.

HISTORY

Skittles has been played in various forms and in numerous countries for hundreds, if not thousands, of years and under different names. In England, the game of skittles has evolved from Kaylepins.
Skittles is played with a set of nine wooden pins and a missile called a cheese, which may roughly be described as a flattened oval of wood weighing between 9–11lb (4–5kg). In Germany and Holland, the cheese is replaced by a large wooden ball and rolled rather than thrown. In the Netherland,s the game is called Dutchpins. While in America it's Ninepins, this game became so popular that in 1899 it was banned as it was thought to be keeping men from their work. A few years later, to get around the law, the game was re-introduced with an additional pin, making the game of Ten Pin Bowling we know today.
See Variations and Rules on page 73 for more details.

Cutting List

PINS

9 pieces 2¹⁵⁄₁₆in x 2¹⁵⁄₁₆in x 10¾in (75mm x 75mm x 275mm) long

BALLS

3 pieces 2¹⁵⁄₁₆in x 2¹⁵⁄₁₆in x 3¾in (75mm x 75mm x 95mm) long

The diameter of the wooden balls will depend upon the size of the pins and the density of the timber, but as a rough guide the diameter will be about the same as the maximum diameter of the pin. I have detailed how to make a template to help get the pins the same and also a sphere turning jig shown on page 21.

I have used European oak (*Quercus robur*) for the pins and sapele (*Entandrophragma cylindricum*) for the three spheres. I chose this timber for no other reason than it is what I found in my stockpile. The finish used was three coats of Danish oil applied off the lathe after all the turning was finished.

ANATOMY OF A SKITTLE PIN

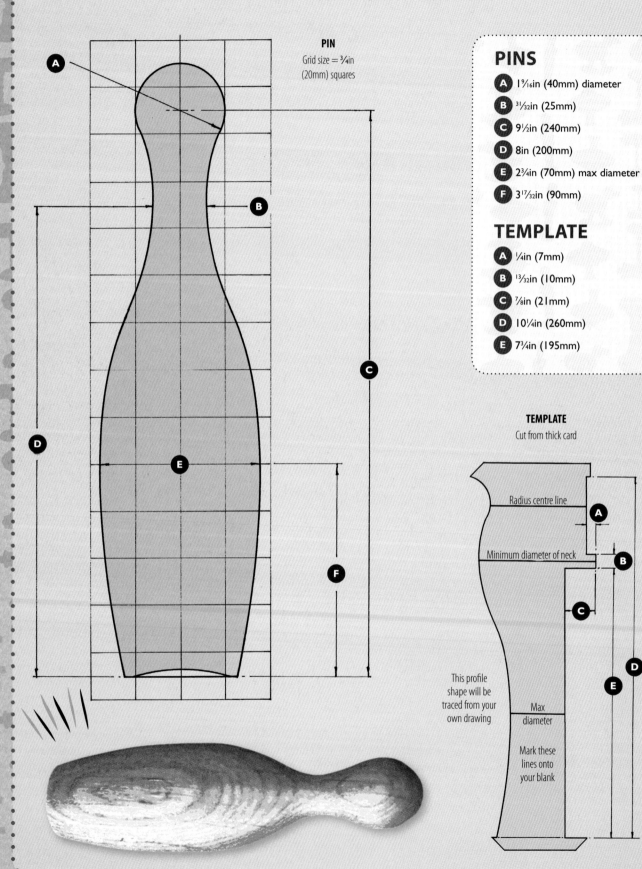

PIN

Grid size = ¾in
(20mm) squares

PINS

A 1⁹⁄₁₆in (40mm) diameter

B 3¹⁄₃₂in (25mm)

C 9½in (240mm)

D 8in (200mm)

E 2¾in (70mm) max diameter

F 3¹⁷⁄₃₂in (90mm)

TEMPLATE

A ¼in (7mm)

B ¹³⁄₃₂in (10mm)

C ⅞in (21mm)

D 10¼in (260mm)

E 7¾in (195mm)

TEMPLATE

Cut from thick card

Radius centre line

Minimum diameter of neck

This profile
shape will be
traced from your
own drawing

Max
diameter

Mark these
lines onto
your blank

PINS

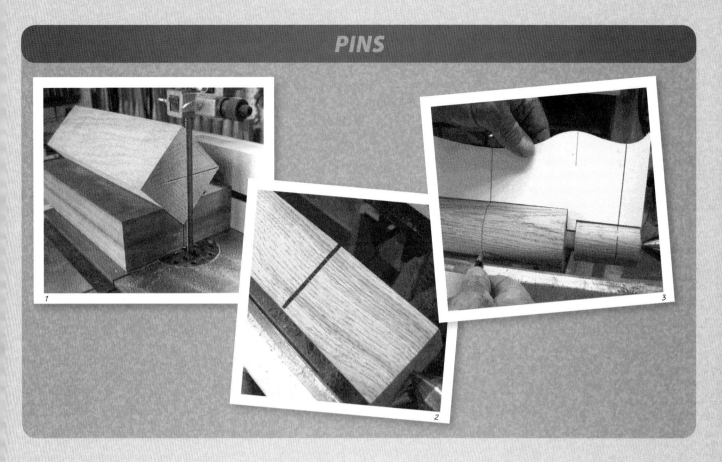

Draw the profile of your skittle using a squared grid as shown opposite. The drawing uses a grid of ¾in (20mm) squares. If you want to make a pin half the size for indoor use, draw the squares at ⅜in (10mm).

PINS

1 Prepare the nine blanks according to the cutting list. When cutting the blanks on the band saw, you can also mark the centres at each end by placing the blank in a sled on the saw which holds the blank at 45°. Make a kerf line from corner to corner, then rotate the blank 90° to mark the other diagonal. Do this at both ends and you can go straight to the lathe **1** .

2 Mount the blank between centres and turn down to a 2⅞in (72mm) diameter cylinder, using a roughing gouge **2** .

3 Use a parting tool to cut a shoulder at each end to give a length of 10¼in (260mm) for the pin. Mark a pencil line around the blank 2⁹⁄₁₆in (65mm) from the top face and reduce the diameter to 1⅝in (42mm) between this line and the top edge. Still using the parting tool, undercut the shoulder to a diameter of 1⅛in (28mm) to indicate the minimum diameter at the neck. Using the template on page 68 will not only save measuring every time you turn a pin, it will also ensure simple errors don't occur as you become faster and more confident **3** . All the above dimensions give a bit of allowance for refining the surface finish later.

4 Transfer the lines from the template onto the blank. These indicate the maximum diameter of the body and the radius line for the top of the pin. Cut a 2in (50mm) diameter at the base of the pin with a parting tool to help define the shape.

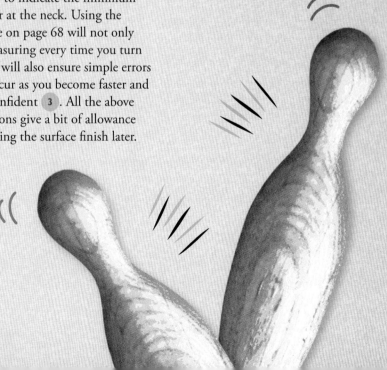

TOP TIP

When you need to turn a square blank down to a cylinder, watch the top edge of the blank. This will appear as a ghost line (A) that gradually becomes solid as the four corners are removed. It can then be difficult to distinguish exactly when the flat faces have all been removed. Draw a line around the square blank and then turn down to a cylinder (B). The line will remain visible, even with just a tiny piece left, and is easier to see (C).

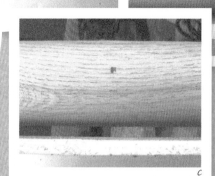

A

C

TOP TIP

One of the skittles will need to be marked in some way to indicate that it is the king pin. This can be done in any number of ways, either by making a cap of contrasting timber, painting the top or cutting in some lines with the long point of a skew chisel (A) and scorching with a hot wire as shown (B).

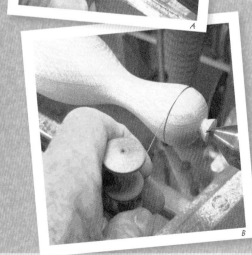

A

B

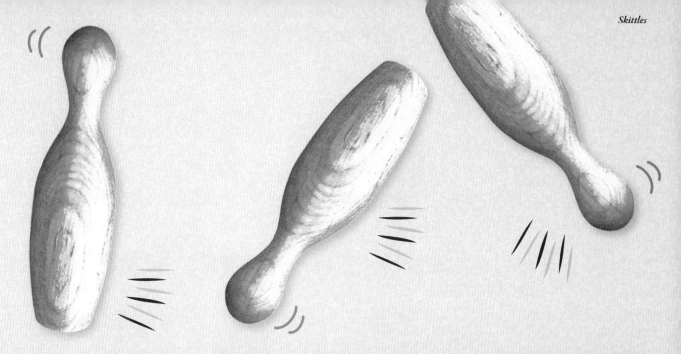

PINS

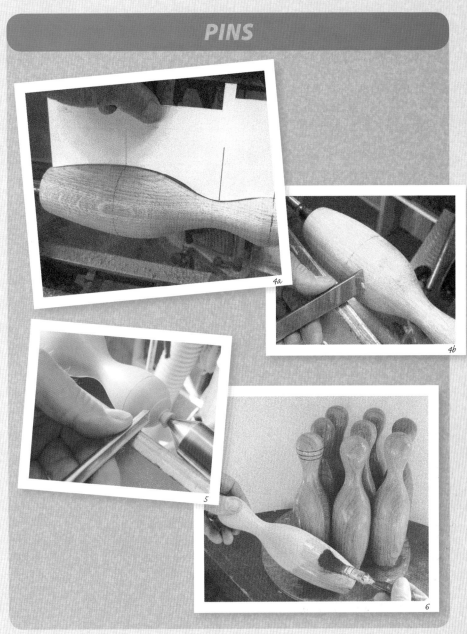

5 Start to form the profile using a roughing gouge, keeping an eye on the progress using the other side of the template. Do not remove the pencil lines, but ensure the profile flows together nicely **4a** . The surface will be quite rough at this stage, but when you are happy with the shape you can refine the surface with a light cut using a skew or spindle gouge **4b** . Oak has a severe blunting effect on tools, so sharpen your chisels frequently to get the best finish.

6 Use a small spindle gouge to form the top of the pin **5** . Sand the whole profile as necessary down to about 400 grit.

7 Reduce the waste at each end and make sure you form a generous concave to the bottom profile so that the pin will stand easily. Remove from the lathe and cut off the waste. Make sure not to pull out the end grain when cutting off. Hand sand the profile to blend in the shape.

8 Make another eight pins (without the marks) before applying three coats of Danish oil or the finish of your choice **6** .

WOODEN BALLS

1 Mount the blank between centres and turn down to a 2¾in (70mm) diameter cylinder.

2 Use a parting tool to cut a ¾in (20mm) diameter spigot at each end of the blank. Use callipers to leave the width of the body of the blank at the same dimension as the diameter. This is the starting point for cutting a sphere **1**. If you are going to use the sphere turning jig, then now is the time to fit it. Follow the guide on page 25 to complete the shape.

3 Alternatively, mark a pencil line around the centre of the blank and with a spindle gouge start to turn the radiused ends. Keep your eye on the top edge of the profile and try to form a true radius as the tool moves from the diameter to the axis point **2a**. Use a simple template to check the progress **2b**. Sand the finished profile down to 400 grit. Reduce the waste to as small as safely possible and remove the blank from the lathe. Cut off the waste and sand to blend in the profile **3**.

4 Apply three coats of Danish oil or the finish of your choice.

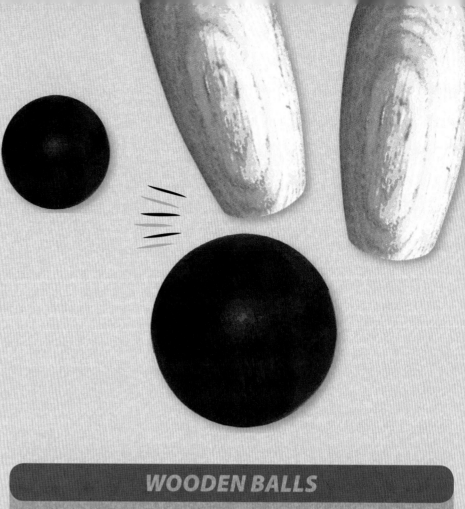

WOODEN BALLS

1

2a

2b

3

RULES

Skittles may be played indoors or outdoors. Different countries have different rules and there are also a number of different games.

Usually, nine wooden pins are set upright in a square with three pins on each side. A corner angle is presented to the player who stands about 6½ yards (6m) away and aims to knock down the pins with a wooden ball. The player is allowed to take one step beyond the delivery line. The game can be played by one person or any number of players in teams.

The ball is thrown an agreed number of times to clear the board. The player who floors all the pins with the least number of throws is the winner.

Another popular form of the game is to have one throw. The players score one point for each pin floored. The pin must be lying on its side; if it leans on another it does not count. To floor all nine pins with one throw, a certain pin must be hit first. This is the skill that can be developed.

In Holland, Dutchpins is played with the middle or king pin marked. There are two alternative ways to play this game. One is to floor the king pin without touching the other eight. The alternative is to knock over the eight pins without touching the king.

Another game uses only four pins, one at each corner. The player who knocks over the four in the least number of throws is the winner. You can also decide whether to have one throw only or an agreed number of throws or points. Each pin floored counts as one point or a value marked on the pin beforehand.

VARIATIONS

In addition to the various games that can be played, there are many different shapes and sizes you can make. Just a few are shown here.

You can make the pins as elaborate or as simple as you like. The skill for you will be in turning nine identical pins and three perfect spheres. The skill for others will be hitting the one particular pin which will knock over all nine.

Skipping rhyme

Children love to skip and as they do, they invariably chant rhymes. The origins of these are now mainly lost in time:

Up and down the ladder wall,
Ha'penny loaf to feed us all,
A bit for you and a bit for me,
And a bit for Punch and Judy.

SKIPPING ROPE

Skipping ropes are one of the oldest toys and were probably dreamt up by children themselves, picking up a piece of discarded rope and learning to skip. The ends of the rope were simply knotted.

Handles started to appear in the early twentieth century, but even these were adapted from wooden spools or bobbins originally used in the woollen mills of the industrial north. The handles quickly caught on as they made the rope much easier to hold.

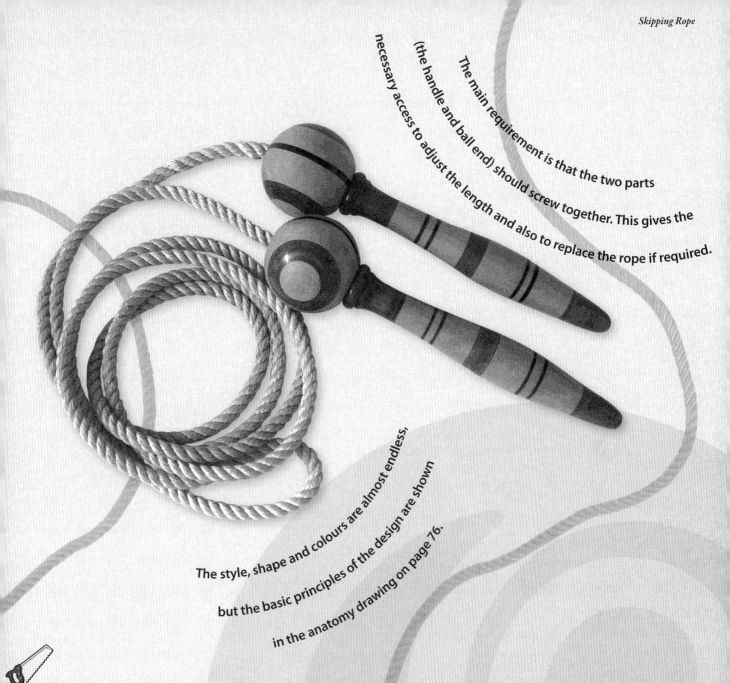

The main requirement is that the two parts (the handle and ball end) should screw together. This gives the necessary access to adjust the length and also to replace the rope if required.

The style, shape and colours are almost endless, but the basic principles of the design are shown in the anatomy drawing on page 76.

Cutting List

HANDLE

2 pieces 1³⁄₁₆in x 1³⁄₁₆in x 7in
(30mm x 30mm x 175mm) long

BALL END

2 pieces 1³¹⁄₃₂in x 1³¹⁄₃₂in x 1³¹⁄₃₂in
(50mm x 50mm x 50mm)
See the drawing on page 76.

In addition to the above, you will need a length of ⁹⁄₃₂in (7mm) diameter rope, about 8ft (2.5m) long (depending on the child's age) and a piece of string or twine to secure the rope in the handle.

The wood chosen for this project will need to be one that can take a hand chased thread. In the example shown here, I am using genero lemonwood (*Calycophyllum multiflorum*) also called castelo boxwood. This is not to be confused with European boxwood (*Buxus sempervirens*), but is an acceptable substitute for this project.

Lemonwood is fine textured, wonderful to work with and takes a good finish straight from the tool. It will produce a crisp thread and, because the grain figure is minimal, makes an ideal base for some additional decoration.

A word of caution, lemonwood will heat check fairly readily if you work with blunt drills or sand aggressively. The finish chosen is an acrylic sanding sealer followed by some decorative rings applied with the piece on the lathe then a final coat of acrylic lacquer.

ANATOMY OF A SKIPPING ROPE

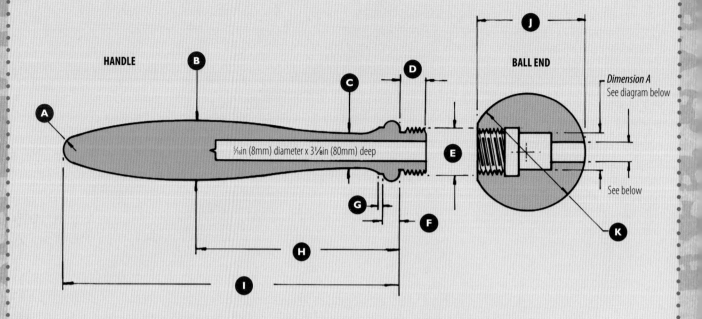

HANDLE

⁵⁄₁₆in (8mm) diameter x 3¹⁄₈in (80mm) deep

BALL END

Dimension A
See diagram below

See below

BLANK

Dimension A *

* Measure the root (smallest) diameter of the thread cut in the handle and drill or cut this diameter just a little smaller

Drill this hole ³⁄₆₄in (1mm) larger than the diameter of your rope

Dotted line indicates diameter of finished turning

Grain direction

The drilling of this blank must be carried out on the lathe in the manner described in the text. This will ensure the concentricity essential for thread chasing

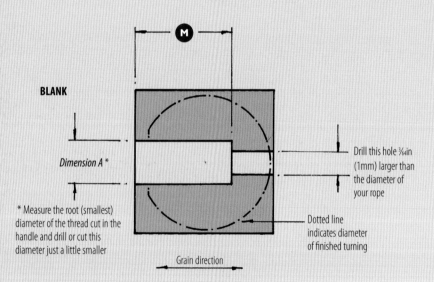

HANDLE

- **A** ³⁄₁₆in (5mm) radius
- **B** ³¹⁄₃₂in (25mm) max diameter
- **C** ¹⁹⁄₃₂in (15mm)
- **D** ¹³⁄₃₂in (10mm)
- **E** ²³⁄₃₂in (18mm) x 16tpi
- **F** ¼in (6mm) bead x ³¹⁄₃₂in (25mm) diameter
- **G** ⁵⁄₆₄in (2mm) x ¾in (19mm) diameter
- **H** 3¹⁷⁄₃₂in (90mm)
- **I** 5²⁹⁄₃₂in (150mm)

BALL END

- **J** 1²³⁄₃₂in (44mm)
- **K** ⁵⁄₁₆in (8mm) diameter

BLANK

- **M** 1³⁄₈in (35mm)

HANDLE

HANDLE

1 Mark the centres at each end of the blank and mount directly in the compression jaws of a long nosed chuck. Drill a hole to accommodate the size of rope you are using. In this example, I am using $\frac{9}{32}$in (7mm) diameter rope and will therefore need a $\frac{5}{16}$in (8mm) diameter hole. Drill to a depth of $3\frac{1}{8}$in (80mm). This could also be done on a drill stand if you prefer. This hole will enable you to use a slightly longer line than is first needed, so you can adjust the length as the child grows, rather than having to replace the whole rope **1** .

2 Mount the blank between centres with the tailstock in the hole you've just drilled, and rough down to a diameter of $\frac{31}{32}$in (25mm) **2** .

3 Mark pencil lines around the blank to indicate the positions of the bead, maximum and minimum diameter and the overall length. Leave enough room at the tailstock end to get your thread chaser to work in **3** .

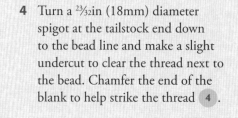

4 Turn a ²³⁄₃₂in (18mm) diameter spigot at the tailstock end down to the bead line and make a slight undercut to clear the thread next to the bead. Chamfer the end of the blank to help strike the thread ④.

5 Slow the speed right down and chase a 16tpi (threads per inch) thread onto the end of the handle ⑤.

6 Rough out the shape of the handle to the lines drawn previously and refine with a sharp chisel ⑥.

7 Reduce the thread length to ¹³⁄₃₂in (10mm) using a narrow parting tool. Only cut through if you are supporting the handle ⑦. If you are not happy to do this, then finish the cut off the lathe later. Adjust the tailstock support as necessary before sanding down the profile. Take care not to remove the crispness of the tooled finish. Seal the handle with several thin coats of acrylic sanding sealer, flatting down between each coat.

8 Reduce the drive spigot to as small as safely possible and remove from the lathe.

9 Cut off the waste at each end as required and sand to match the profile. Seal the ends.

HANDLE

TOP TIP

Use some paste wax to lubricate the work and to make cutting the thread easier.

BALL END

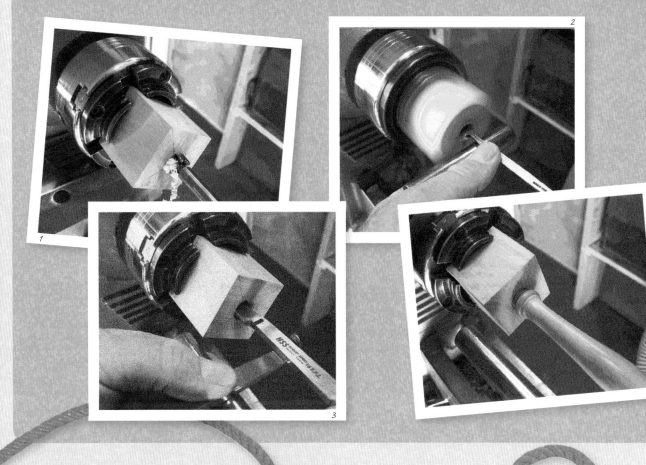

BALL END

1. Mount the cube directly in the jaws of a compression chuck with the direction of grain along the axis.

2. Measure the root (smallest) diameter of the thread cut on the handle and drill a slightly smaller hole into the blank. The root diameter in my case measures ⅝in (16mm). The nearest drill bit I have below this is ⁹⁄₁₆in (14mm). Remember that a blunt or a badly sharpened drill will tend to cut oversize. If you are not sure of the actual cutting diameter, use a test piece and measure it.

   Use a well-sharpened saw tooth bit and drill slowly to a depth of 1⅜in (35mm) into the end grain. You may need to use a scraper to resize the hole after drilling to suit your own circumstances **1**.

3. Drill a ⁵⁄₁₆in (8mm) diameter hole through the blank, see the drawing on page 76.

4. Cut a recess to clear the thread, leaving a ²⁵⁄₃₂in (20mm) length on which to chase the thread. Form a slight bevel at the open end **2**.

5. Slow the speed down and chase a 16tpi thread inside the blank. The mark on the chaser indicates the depth of thread. In this case there is plenty of room before hitting the bottom of the hole **3**.

6. Keep trying the handle to check your progress **4**.

BALL END

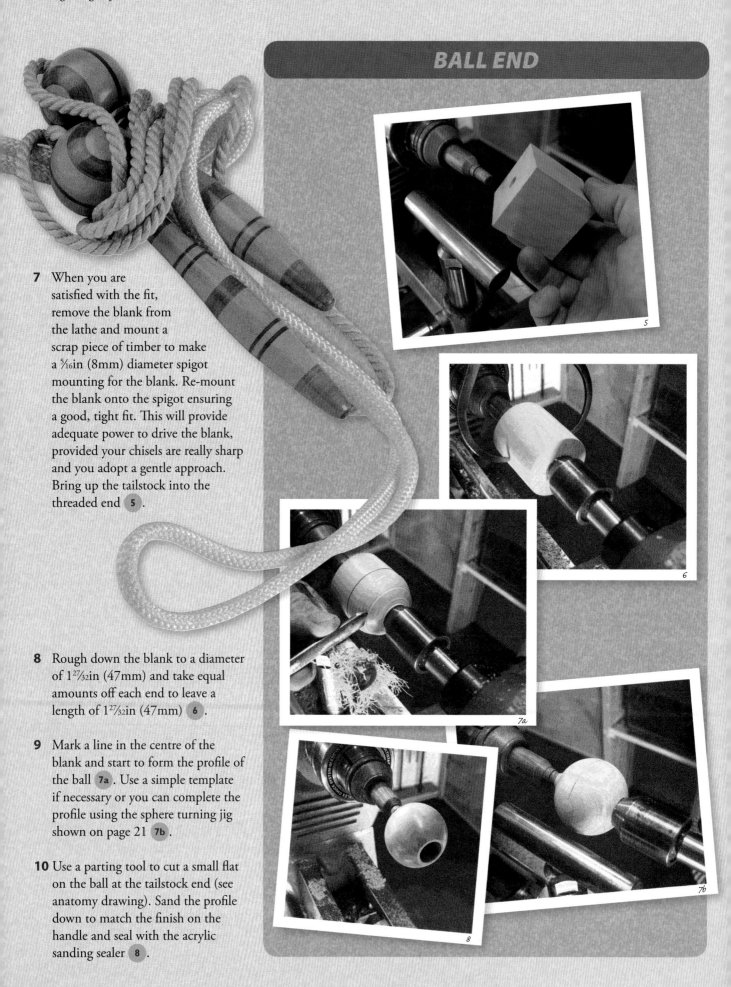

7 When you are satisfied with the fit, remove the blank from the lathe and mount a scrap piece of timber to make a ⁵⁄₁₆in (8mm) diameter spigot mounting for the blank. Re-mount the blank onto the spigot ensuring a good, tight fit. This will provide adequate power to drive the blank, provided your chisels are really sharp and you adopt a gentle approach. Bring up the tailstock into the threaded end **5** .

8 Rough down the blank to a diameter of 1²⁷⁄₃₂in (47mm) and take equal amounts off each end to leave a length of 1²⁷⁄₃₂in (47mm) **6** .

9 Mark a line in the centre of the blank and start to form the profile of the ball **7a** . Use a simple template if necessary or you can complete the profile using the sphere turning jig shown on page 21 **7b** .

10 Use a parting tool to cut a small flat on the ball at the tailstock end (see anatomy drawing). Sand the profile down to match the finish on the handle and seal with the acrylic sanding sealer **8** .

DECORATION

If you want to decorate the items while they are on the lathe, leave the ball end mounted on the spigot and screw in the handle. Bring up the tailstock and use a short length of plastic sleeve or a little concave button, fitted between the handle end and the tailstock point, to prevent marking.

1 Reduce the speed to about 100rpm and use a brush or felt tip pen to mark the decorative rings onto the handle as required.

2 Paint the ball end in a similar way or if you wish to apply the rings at another angle, remount the ball end between two small pads at the angle required and paint on the rings. Use only toy safe paint and leave to dry.

FINISHING

When all the paint is dry, apply two or three coats of acrylic lacquer.

FITTING THE ROPE

Nearly all the ropes sold today are synthetic and sold according to the diameter.

I have used $\frac{9}{32}$in (7mm) diameter rope. The length needed will depend on the age of the child, although a 8ft (2.5m) length will fit most. Experiment to get the best length for the child concerned. As a rough guide, I found that a length between handles of 72in (1.8m) was about right for my eight-year-old granddaughter. The rope can be cut with a hot blade which will also seal the end as it cuts to prevent it fraying.

Thread the rope through the ball ends and use the string or twine to tie a knot around the rope to prevent it pulling out when in use **1** . This also allows some adjustment in the future. Screw on the handles and it's finished.

FITTING THE ROPE

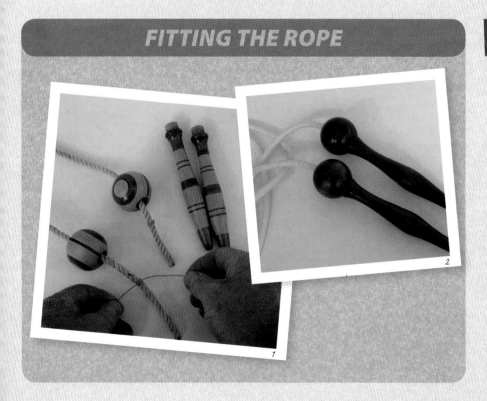

VARIATIONS

The style, shape, size and colour of the handles are almost limitless, as are the colours and weave of the ropes. A good place to buy ropes from is a boat chandlers as there is normally a huge selection in all colours and sizes.

You can even considerably extend the range of timbers used beyond those which would normally be considered as suitable for taking a thread, by making up small inserts out of boxwood and gluing these into the blanks **2** .

Small bells or ribbons can also be tied to the handles to add interest, colour or individuality to the finished toy.

BALL AND CUP

This toy, like the yo-yo, seems to have originated in China. It wasn't until the eighteenth century that it became popular in France, where it was known as *Bilboquet*.

It is one of those timeless toys that can't be much improved upon, although there are various ways to make the game more difficult. The toy is an ideal opportunity to demonstrate your turning skills and, even if it's only made for show, is an interesting piece of treen.

Cutting List

BALL
1 piece 1⅞in x 1⅞in x 1⅞in
(48mm x 48mm x 48mm)

CUP
1 piece 2⁹⁄₁₆in x 2⁹⁄₁₆in x 2³⁄₁₆in
(65mm x 65mm x 55mm) long

HANDLE
1 piece ³¹⁄₃₂in x ³¹⁄₃₂in x 7in
(25mm x 25mm 175mm) long

Any well-seasoned hardwood will do.
I've used mahogany (*Khaya ivorensis*) for
the cup and handle and American black
walnut (*Juglans nigra*) for the ball. I have
found that the cup and handle look
better when made from the same type
of timber. In addition to the above, you
will need a piece of string about 15in
(40cm) long.

ANATOMY OF A CUP AND BALL

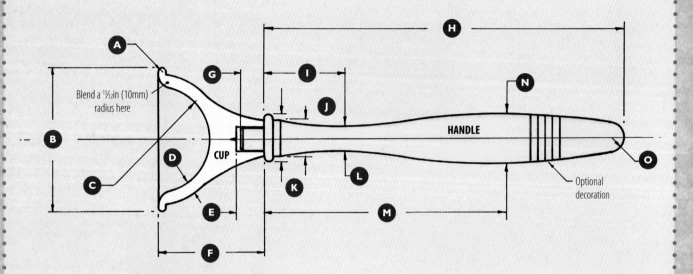

Blend a ¹³⁄₃₂in (10mm) radius here

CUP

HANDLE

Optional decoration

BALL

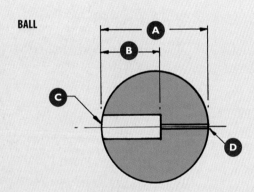

TEMPLATE

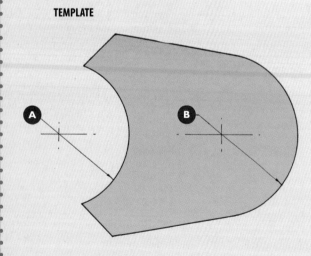

CUP

A ⁵⁄₆₄in (2mm) radius

B 2¹¹⁄₃₂in (60mm) diameter

C ¹⁵⁄₁₆in (24mm) radius

D ⁵⁄₃₂in (4mm)

E ³⁄₈in (10mm) diameter x ¹⁵⁄₃₂in (12mm) deep hole

F 1³¹⁄₃₂in (50mm)

HANDLE

G ³⁄₈in (10mm) diameter x ³⁄₈in (10mm) long spigot

H 6¼in (160mm)

I 1⁹⁄₁₆in (40mm)

J ²⁵⁄₃₂in (20mm) diameter x ⅛in (3mm)

K ³¹⁄₃₂in (25mm) diameter x ⅛in (3mm) wide bead

L ¹⁹⁄₃₂in (15mm) diameter

M 4¹¹⁄₃₂in (110mm)

N 2⁹⁄₃₂in (23mm) diameter

O ³⁄₁₆in (5mm) radius

BALL

A 1¾in (44mm) diameter

B ³¹⁄₃₂in (25mm)

C ³⁄₈in (10mm) diameter

D ³⁄₃₂in (2mm) diameter hole

TEMPLATE

A ⅞in (22mm) radius

B ¹⁵⁄₁₆in (24mm) radius

If you are turning the ball by hand, and not using the sphere turning jig, then you will find the template very useful. Copy the dimensions onto a thick piece of card and cut out using a sharp knife.

BALL

I've started with the ball for two reasons, it can be used as a gauge when making the cup and also as a chuck as you will see later.

1 Mark the diagonals on the end grain of the 1⅞in (48mm) cube. Drill a ⅜in (10mm) diameter hole x ³¹⁄₃₂in (25mm) deep into one end and a ³⁄₃₂in (2mm) diameter hole into the other through to the first hole **1** .

2 Mount a piece of scrap timber in a suitable chuck and turn a ⅜in (10mm) diameter x 1³⁄₁₆in (30mm) long spigot **2a** . Push the pre-drilled blank onto the spigot. It should be a nice tight fit. Bring up the tailstock into the ³⁄₃₂in (2mm) diameter hole in the cube **2b** .

3 Reduce the cube to a cylinder with the roughing gouge, just removing any flat surfaces. Square up the ends with a parting chisel so the length of the cylinder is exactly the same as the diameter **3a** . Mark a pencil line halfway along the length **3b** .

BALL

TOP TIP

If you prefer, you can turn the ball using the sphere turning jig shown on page 21, and refer to turning spheres described on page 25.

BALL

4a

4b

4 Turning the ball by hand should not present any problems because, unlike other spheres in other projects, this one has a hole through it and is therefore easier to hold. Start at one end and begin shaping the curve, gradually working towards the revolving centre **4a** . Try to form the curve in a uniform manner, removing wood evenly on both the front and end surfaces. Use the template to check that you are forming the perfect sphere **4b** .

5 When you are satisfied with the profile, hand sand through the grits before applying sanding sealer. Leaving the ball on the jig, either remove the jig from the chuck marking the jaw positions for re-mounting later, or remove the chuck, jig and ball as one.

CUP

1 Mark diagonals across the end grain and drill a hole x $^{25}/_{32}$in (20mm) deep in one end to suit a screw chuck **1** . Mount the blank onto the screw chuck and rough down to a cylinder with the roughing gouge. Square up the ends with a parting chisel.

2 Fit a Jacobs-type chuck in the tailstock quill and drill a $^3/_8$in (10mm) diameter x $^{15}/_{32}$in (12mm) deep hole in the centre of the tailstock end **2** .

3 Turn a dovetail to suit the compression jaws of your chuck. This should be about $1^{31}/_{32}$in (50mm) diameter **3a** . Then reverse mount the blank. Hollow out the centre of the blank using a spindle gouge with a short bevel **3b** (see anatomy drawing). The depth of the hollow will be $^{31}/_{32}$in (25mm).

4 The diameter of the cup needs to be about $^3/_{16}$in (5mm) larger than the diameter of the ball. Check your progress with the template to ensure that you are forming a nicely rounded hollow **4** .

5 Make sure the ball fits loosely and does not jam inside **5** . Use a rounded scraper to refine the shape as necessary, then sand, seal and finish. I've chosen an antique paste wax finish. Remove from the lathe.

6 Re-mount the ball, jig and chuck assembly. Fit the cup over the ball with a small off-cut of router mat or other non-slip material between the ball and cup **6a**. Bring the tailstock up into the ⅜in (10mm) diameter hole and finish turning the profile **6b** (see the anatomy drawing). Sand and seal as required. Before removing the cup, square up and slightly undercut the small end with a skew chisel **6c**. This will ensure a close fitting joint. Apply the finish of your choice and remove the cup from the lathe. Apply the finish to the previously sealed ball while it is on the lathe **6d**.

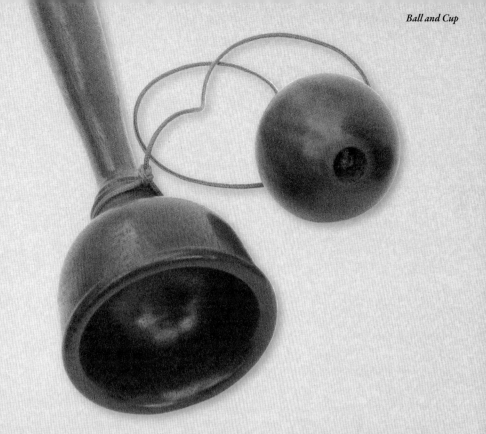

CUP

HANDLE

1 This is where you can really go to town and demonstrate your skill. I have chosen a simple profile to show the main requirements, but you can turn any profile you like.

2 Mark the diagonals on the ends of the blank and mount between the centres, turn down to a cylinder **1** .

3 Define the position of the bead at the top of the handle and form a ⅜in (10mm) diameter spigot x ⅜in (10mm) long to fit the cup **2** (see anatomy drawing).

4 Turn the remainder of the profile using a large spindle gouge or skew chisel and refine the bead **3** .

5 Apply some decoration using a skew or small point tool **4a** . Sand and seal as required and apply your finish. Reduce the mounting spigot to as small as safely possible and remove from the lathe **4b** .

6 Cut off the remaining pip with a sharp blade, sand down the end and apply the finish.

7 Check the fit of the cup and handle, then glue the two parts together.

8 Finally, thread the string through the ball and tie a knot on the end. Pull the knot back into the larger hole and tie the other end around the handle. You are now ready to play.

HANDLE

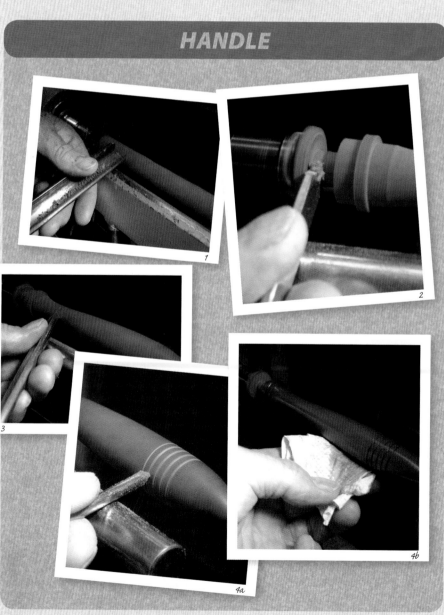

HOW TO PLAY

Take the handle by the middle. The ball should be thrown upwards by a slight jerk of the wrist, not the whole arm. If done properly, it falls of its own accord into the cup.

The next feature is to swing the ball into the cup. A good player should be able to catch the ball in the cup with their eyes shut.

You can also make the game considerably more difficult in a number of ways (see Variations).

VARIATIONS

The game can be made more difficult, either by reducing the cup size or increasing the diameter of the ball. The bilboquet shown is a copy of a nineteenth century one I saw at an antiques auction. The ball is 2¾in (70mm) diameter and the cup is 1⅞in (48mm) diameter with a very shallow hollow. Furthermore, the end of the handle has a ⁵⁄₁₆in (8mm) diameter turned spigot x 1³¹⁄₃₂in (50mm) long, so if you find the conventional game too easy you can try to catch the ball on the spigot.

The secret of success is to give the ball a smart spin with the fingers of your free hand. Let it spin as far as it can in one direction and allow it to spin back again ten or eleven times. Watch that it is quite steady, then throw it up as before. Turn the point upwards, as if you were aiming at the spot where the string enters the ball, and just as the ball touches the point, let your hand sink slightly. The best of luck!

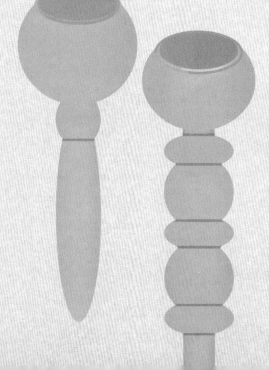

WOODPECKER

It is very difficult to ignore this little chap, just looking at him makes you want to set him in motion and then watch as he pecks his way to the bottom of the pole. The natural action of the toy lends itself to being a woodpecker, but there are many variations you can make.

There are a couple of items of hardware to obtain and it would be sensible to get these before starting this project as the dimensions of the holes may differ slightly depending on what you are able to acquire.

Since the really good hardware stores have become a rarity and it is now more difficult to obtain things like springs of a certain size or rate, I have opted instead to use curtain wire. This is the plastic covered coil of spring steel used for holding up net curtains, bought by the yard (metre) from curtain shops and therefore readily available. Strip off the plastic coating and you will have a length of very handy spring steel.

The other item to obtain is 16in (400mm) of ⅛in (2–3mm) diameter brass rod. Any smooth rod will do and can be found at your local DIY store or motor accessory shop sold as brazing rod. Whatever material you acquire for this project, measure it carefully and adjust the measurement given in the text to suit your own application.

Cutting List

BODY, CAP AND COLLAR
1 piece $^{31}/_{32}$in x $^{31}/_{32}$in x $5^{29}/_{32}$in
(25mm x 25mm x 150mm) long

BASE
1 piece $2^{9}/_{16}$in x $2^{9}/_{16}$in x $^{31}/_{32}$in
(65mm x 65mm x 25mm) thick

BEAK
1 piece ¼in x ¼in x $^{31}/_{32}$in
(6mm x 6mm x 25mm) long

In addition to the above, you will need a $1^{11}/_{32}$in (34mm) long spring (compression or tension) about ⅛in (3mm) in diameter, a 16in (400mm) length of ⅛in (2–3mm) diameter brass rod (see notes above) and one coloured feather.

For this project I've used afrormosia (*Pericopsis elata*) for the body, cap, collar and base. I used amarello (*Aspidosperma peroba*) for the beak as it is such a distinct yellow colour, although any hardwood will do. This is a good project for using up some small off cuts. The finish I've chosen is a commercial friction polish on top of a sanding sealer.

TOP TIP

Try to ensure that the two holes drilled for the spring provide a tight fit. This will make tuning up easier, which is done before gluing.

ANATOMY OF WOODPECKER

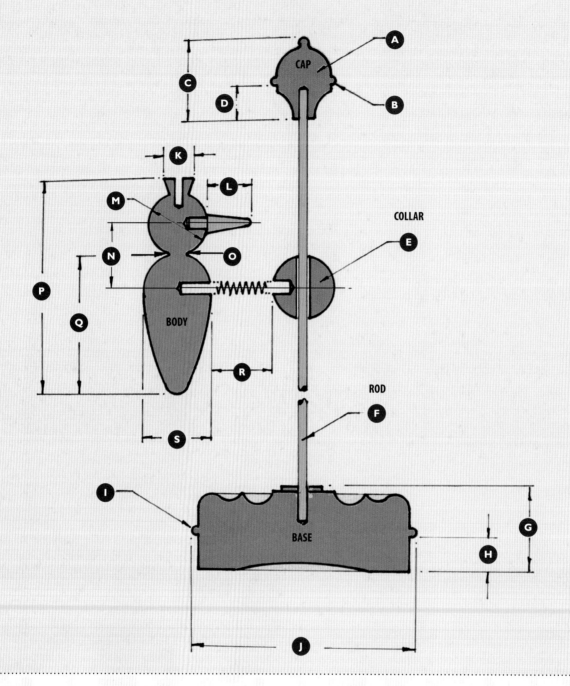

CAP
A ²⁵⁄₃₂in (20mm) diameter

B ⁵⁄₆₄in (2mm)

C ³¹⁄₃₂in (25mm)

D ¹⁵⁄₃₂in (12mm)

COLLAR
E ²⁵⁄₃₂in (20mm) diameter

ROD
F ⅛in (2-3mm) diameter x 16in (400mm)

BASE
G ²⁹⁄₃₂in (23mm)

H ¹³⁄₃₂in (10mm)

I ⁵⁄₆₄in (2mm) bead

J 2⁷⁄₁₆in (62mm) diameter

BODY
K ¹¹⁄₃₂in (9mm)

L ½in (13mm)

M ²⁵⁄₃₂in (20mm) diameter

N ²⁵⁄₃₂in (20mm) centres

O ¹³⁄₃₂in (10mm) diameter

P 2⁹⁄₁₆in (65mm)

Q 1⁹⁄₁₆in (40mm)

R ²³⁄₃₂in (18mm) approx.

S ⅞in (22mm) diameter

The body, capping piece and collar are all turned from the one piece of $^{31}/_{32}$in x $^{31}/_{32}$in x $5^{29}/_{32}$in (25mm x 25mm x 150mm) long timber. Mark the diagonals on the ends to find the centres and indent with a bradawl. Mount the blank between centres on the lathe and turn down to a cylinder, just removing any flat surfaces.

CAP

1 You will need to fit a protective cap on top of the pole, for safety and appearance. A simple piece of decoration looks good. Fit the roughed down cylinder directly into a compression chuck, square up the end and drill a hole to match the diameter of your rod x $^{19}/_{32}$in (15mm) deep into the end **1a**.

2 Bring up the tailstock into the hole and turn the profile of the cap. Sand, seal and finish before removing the tailstock and parting off from the lathe. Put the part to one side safely for final assembly **1b**.

CAP

1a

1b

COLLAR

2

3

COLLAR

1 Square up the end and drill a hole $^{1}/_{64}$in ($^{1}/_{2}$mm) larger than the rod diameter x $1^{3}/_{8}$in (35mm) deep. Bring the tailstock up for support and mark a line $^{25}/_{32}$in (20mm) from the end. Then using a parting tool, undercut the diameter to $^{13}/_{32}$in (10mm).

2 Form the profile of the collar (see anatomy drawing). Sand, seal and finish as necessary, then remove the tailstock centre before parting off. Remember that the centre has a hole through it **2**.

3 Drill a hole in the centre of the collar at right angles to the rod hole to suit your spring x $^{1}/_{4}$in (6mm) deep. Use the rod to hold the collar while drilling and a simple jig (see notes on drilling spheres on page 14) to keep everything steady **3**.

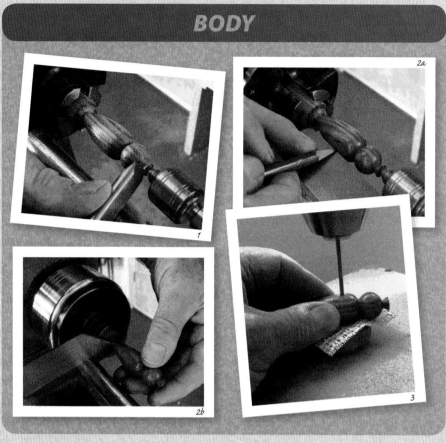

BODY

BODY

1 Check you have enough material clear of the chuck to form the body, bring up the tailstock again into the end hole drilled previously. Mark a line to indicate the neck area and form the profile using a small spindle gouge. Make sure to form the head at the tailstock end. The hole in the end is for the feather. Leave enough support at the drive end to work on the main part of the profile. Use the long point of a skew chisel to square up the top of the crown **1** .

2 Decide where the front of the body will be, this will depend on the grain pattern or other markings, usually the centre of a growth ring is ideal. Mark a line to indicate the axis using the tool rest if necessary. Then mark two radial lines for the hole centres, one in the centre of the head for the beak and one in the body for the spring **2a** , (see anatomy drawing). Mark the hole centres using a bradawl before sanding, sealing and finishing as required. Turn the remainder of the profile before parting off **2b** . Sand the base of the profile to match, apply sealer and finish as necessary.

3 Drill a ⁵⁄₃₂in (4mm) diameter hole x ¼in (6mm) deep in the centre of the head for the beak and a hole in the front of the body to suit the diameter of your spring x ¹³⁄₃₂in (10mm) deep **3** .

BASE

1 Mark the diagonals to find the centre and scribe a 2¹⁷⁄₃₂in (64mm) diameter circle in pencil. Cut off the corners using the band saw **1**. Turn a disc to use as a glue chuck and use a hot melt glue to stick the blank to the disc. Use the centre mark on the blank to line up with the tailstock or cut a hole through the disc and mount the blank in the centre **2**. Mount the blank on your chuck and form a recessed dovetail to fit the expansion jaws of your chuck **3**.

2 Remove the blank from the lathe complete with the glue chuck. Using a chisel, part the items. Remount the base on the expansion jaws of your chuck. Turn the outside edge down to 2⁷⁄₁₆in (62mm) diameter. The bead is optional.

3 Fit a Jacobs-type chuck into the tailstock and drill a hole to suit your brass rod x ¹⁹⁄₃₂in (15mm) deep **4**.

4 Either copy the profile shown in the anatomy drawing or design your own pattern. Sand, seal and finish as required **5**.

TOP TIP

For a really good finish, after sanding down to about 600 grit and sealing the wood, use the shavings to polish the surface before applying the finish.

5 Make up a jam chuck or use a small set of cole jaws. Reverse mount the blank to work on the bottom **6**. Protect the finish by wrapping the turning in masking tape or cling film. Use a gouge to form a slightly concave base so the toy will sit without wobbling. Sand, seal and finish.

BASE

BEAK

1 Turn the beak from a piece of different timber than the body (see anatomy drawing). Sand, seal and finish as required. Part off from the lathe and sand the tip so it is not too sharp.

ROD

1 Make sure the piece of rod is smooth and straight. Cut to a length of 16in (400mm) and clean or degrease as necessary.

SPRING

1 If you are using the curtain wire, you will need a $^{25}/_{32}$in (20mm) length. After cutting, grind off any sharp ends. The tension is much too strong and will need to be weakened. Place one end in a bench vice and, using a pair of pliers, pull open the coils of the spring gently until it measures approximately $1^{11}/_{32}$in (34mm) in length. If you are using your own spring, experiment with the assembly to find the best rate. (See Tuning Up).

ASSEMBLY

1 All the parts are ready for assembly 〔1〕. Glue Woody's beak and feather in place, then glue the rod into the base. Place the collar on the rod, making sure it will drop freely to the bottom. It must be loose enough to drop straight down. Push the spring into the collar on one end and the body on the other. Do not glue the spring into the collar or body yet. If the fit is a bit loose, use some tape or paper to make a tight fit. Glue on the capping piece.

TUNING UP

Slide the assembled body and collar to the top of the rod and, holding Woody's head, slightly deflect the spring down then release. The assembly should now peck its way to the bottom of the rod. Adjust the tension and the length of the spring if necessary until the required action is satisfactory. Glue in both ends of the spring. As a rough guide, the weaker or longer the spring, as well as the smaller the hole in the collar, the slower the action.

ASSEMBLY

You can make any number of variations to this toy. A recent one requested was a monkey stealing a banana from a tree.

I'm afraid that if you bought a metre of curtain wire you will have enough springs for another 49 toys.

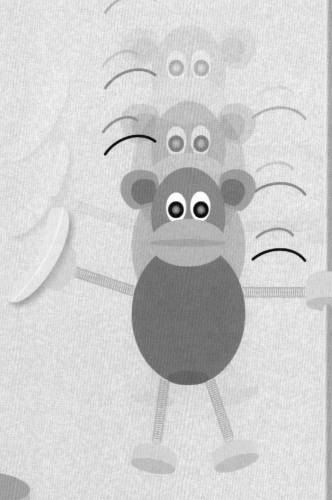

How it Works

The toy works by gravity. When it is at the top of the rod, the weight of the woodpecker pulls the collar at an angle, preventing it from dropping down the rod. When the spring is deflected down and released, the action of the spring on its upward recoil lifts the collar to a vertical position, allowing it to drop slightly until the weight of the woodpecker pulls the collar at an angle again, consequently jamming the movement. The inertia causes the spring to recoil back up to continue the action until Woody gets to the bottom of the rod.

TABLE QUOITS

History

There have been many variations of the game of quoits in different countries over many centuries; in fact, it was one of the five games of the Greek Pentathlon. This table top version was a popular past-time in the Victorian household and remains a favourite to this day. The game can be played by individuals or teams and for any number of points agreed upon. (See Rules).

The turning is quite straightforward, with a nice mix of faceplate and between centres spindle work which is all kept quite plain.

For the quoits themselves, I am going to use a ring-cutting tool. The main reason for this is economy of timber. All the rings can be cut from the circumference of the blank, leaving the core intact for another project.

Ring cutters come in a range of sizes usually in sets of two, but a recent addition to the market is a tool with different size cutters which can be purchased one at a time when needed, to help spread the cost.

Cutting List

PIN
1 piece $3\frac{1}{32}$in x $3\frac{1}{32}$in x $9\frac{1}{2}$in
(25mm x 25mm x 240mm) long

BASE
1 piece $4\frac{15}{16}$in x $4\frac{15}{16}$in x $3\frac{1}{32}$in
(125mm x 125mm x 25mm) thick

BUTTON FEET
1 piece $\frac{7}{8}$in x $\frac{7}{8}$in x $2\frac{15}{16}$in
(22mm x 22mm x 75mm) long
(Makes 3 feet)

QUOITS (10)
1 piece $3\frac{15}{16}$in x $3\frac{15}{16}$in x 8in
(100mm x 100mm x 200mm) long

These cutters are double-sided so only one in each size is required. The ideal wood for a quoit is one in which the grain is interlocked in all directions so that there will be few short grain sections.

There are several timbers which have curly, twisted grain. I have chosen English elm (*Ulmus procera*) since it is readily available. My next choice would be beech (*Fagus sylvatica*) as it's strong enough to make the quoits even with two sections of short grain, but you may need to increase the cross section a little to compensate. To make the quoits easy to identify, five of them will be stained darker prior to sealing.

For the base and pin, I have chosen lemonwood (*Calycophyllum multiflorum*), also called castelo boxwood. The three little button feet are made from one short length of cocobolo (*Dalbergia retusa*). My only reason for using this timber is that I have a piece left over from another project which is too short for its originally intended purchase. Any suitable timber will do.

The quoits are finished with a cellulose sanding sealer followed by two coats of melamine lacquer. The base, pin and feet are sealed and finished with a dark wood friction polish, which gives a nice honey brown tone to the lemonwood.

ANATOMY OF TABLE QUOITS

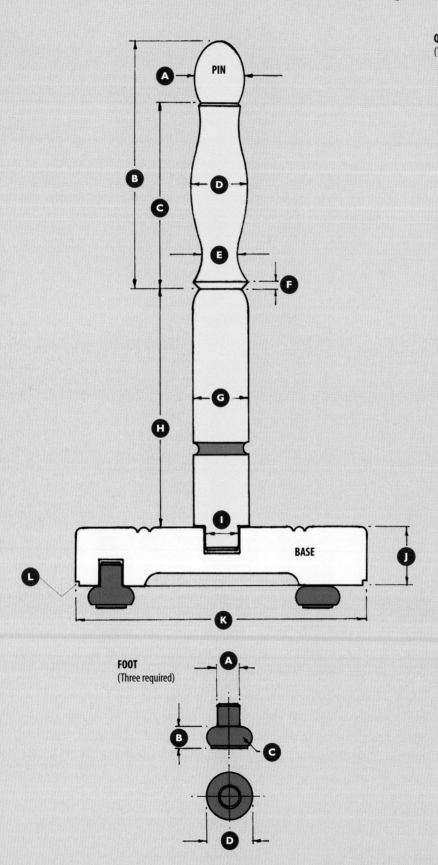

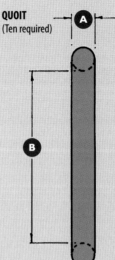

QUOIT
(Ten required)

PIN

BASE

FOOT
(Three required)

PIN AND BASE

A ²⁵⁄₃₂in (20mm) diameter

B 4²³⁄₃₂in (120mm)

C 3¹⁷⁄₃₂in (90mm)

D ²⁹⁄₃₂in (23mm) diameter

E ¹⁹⁄₃₂in (15mm) diameter

F ⅛in (3mm)

G ²⁹⁄₃₂in (23mm) diameter

H 3¾in (95mm)

I ⅝in (15mm) diameter x ⅜in (10mm) long spigot

J ²⁹⁄₃₂in (23mm)

K 4²³⁄₃₂in (120mm)

L ³⁄₆₄in (1mm) square rebate

FOOT

A ⅜in (10mm) diameter x ¼in (6mm) long spigot

B 1³⁄₃₂in (10mm)

C ³⁄₁₆in (5mm) radius

D ²⁵⁄₃₂in (20mm) diameter

QUOIT

A ⅜in (10mm) diameter

B 3¹⁄₁₆in (78mm) diameter

BASE

BASE

1 Mark the diagonals across one face of the blank and then use a compass to scribe a 2⁷⁄₁₆in (62mm) radius from the centre. Drill a hole to suit your screw chuck x ¹⁹⁄₃₂in (15mm) deep **1** .

2 Use the band saw to cut the corners off. Follow the pencil line as a guide, **2** and mount the blank onto the screw chuck.

3 Form a shallow dovetail recess in the centre of the exposed face to match your own expansion chuck **3** .

4 Square up the face with a scraper or your own preferred method and use a straight edge to check it is nice and flat **4** .

5 Reverse mount the blank onto the expansion chuck then square up and flatten this face using a sharp scraper. Use a small scraper to cut a ¹⁹⁄₃₂in (15mm) diameter hole x ⁷⁄₁₆in (11mm) deep in the centre of the blank **5** .

6 Turn the outside edge down to 4²³⁄₃₂in (120mm) diameter **6** .

7 Cut in a small bead or pair of incised rings on a diameter of about 2¾in (70mm). This is optional, but just breaks up the plain surface **7** .

8 Form a small radius to the top edge and sand down to 400 grit, taking care not to spoil the crispness of any detail you turned on the face. Seal the face and edge with a friction polish, one for dark wood gives a honey colour to the rather pale wood. Work quickly here but avoid overheating the timber. Buff up with a paper towel **8** .

9 Reverse mount onto a spigot chuck or your cole jaws and turn a radius to the edge of the dovetail to soften the profile. Form some rings or beads as decoration if required **9** . Cut a ¹⁄₁₆in (1mm) square rebate on the bottom edge.

10 Mark a 3¹⁷⁄₃₂in (90mm) diameter in pencil. Use indexing if you have it or a pair of dividers to mark three equi-spaced centres on the diameter **10** . You may decide to drill the three ⅜in (10mm) diameter x ⁹⁄₃₂in (7mm) deep holes now or do so later using the bench drill which is often easier. I have chosen the bench drill method. Mark the centres of each hole using a bradawl and sand the underside face to remove pencil lines. Finish the bottom face to match the remainder of the turning.

11 When it's all dry, drill three holes for the feet. Use a cloth to protect the finish on the top face **11** .

BASE

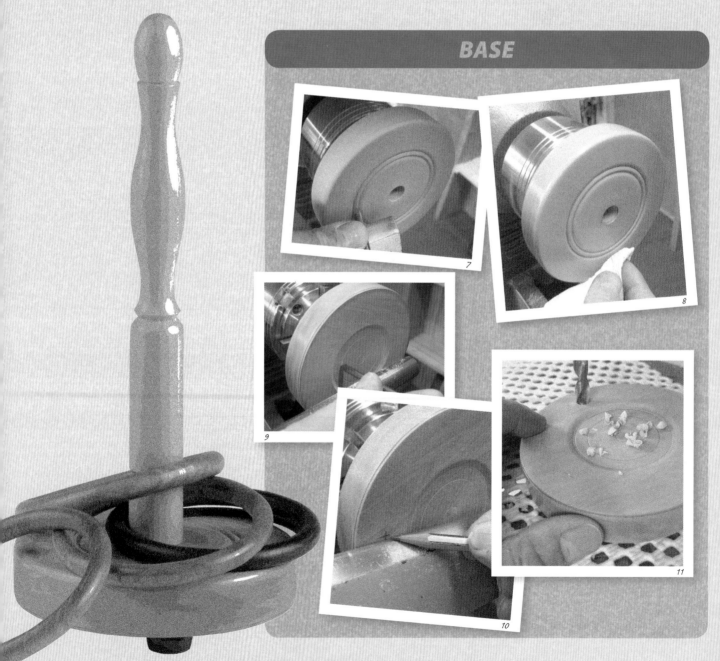

PIN

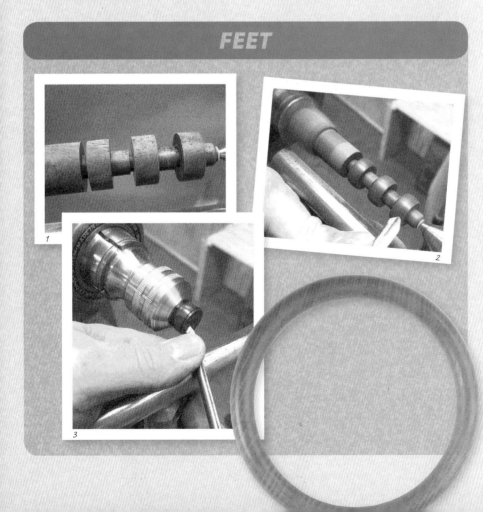

1 Mark the centres of the blank at each end and mount between centres.

2 Turn the blank down to a $^{29}/_{32}$in (23mm) diameter pin **1**.

3 Use a parting tool to block out your design **2**. This can be as simple or as fancy as you like, alternatively follow the profile shown in the anatomy drawing.

4 Reduce the waste to as small as safely possible **3a** and form a spigot $^{19}/_{32}$in (15mm) diameter x $^{11}/_{32}$in (9mm) long to fit the base. Sand and finish to match the base turning **3b**.

FEET

1 Mount the square blank directly into a small compression chuck and bring up the tailstock centre. Rough down a minimum length of $2^{11}/_{32}$in (60mm), just removing the flat surfaces. This will be sufficient to make three feet.

2 Turn down to a $^{25}/_{32}$in (20mm) diameter and use a parting tool to form rough profiles of all three feet **1**. Remember you should allow enough space between each foot for parting off.

3 Form the outside profile and check the $^{3}/_{8}$in (10mm) diameter x $^{1}/_{4}$in (6mm) long spigots **2**. Withdraw the tailstock and use a thin parting tool to cut through and separate each foot.

4 Re-mount the blank in a small compression chuck and finish turning the bottom of the foot. Cut a $^{3}/_{64}$in (1mm) square rebate on the bottom edge to match the base profile **3**. Seal and finish the turning. Repeat for the other feet and place to one side.

QUOITS

1 Mount the blank between centres and turn down to a $3^{27}/_{32}$in (98mm) diameter cylinder.

2 Block out the blank with a parting tool at regular intervals to form square edged sections with enough space between them to allow access for your own particular ring cutter **1** . All ten quoits can be made from this size blank.

3 Gently ease the ring cutter into the side of the square edge section to form one half of the first quoit. Reverse the cutter and form the other half **2a** . With a little practice you will be able to judge the point just before separating the ring from the blank **2b** and be able to sand the outside profile of the quoits before cutting through **2c** .

4 You still need to sand by hand **3** before staining or sealing and finishing. Follow the procedure to make all ten quoits.

ASSEMBLY

1 Refer to the anatomy drawing and glue the feet into the base. Glue in the pin.

QUOITS

1

2a

2b

2c

3

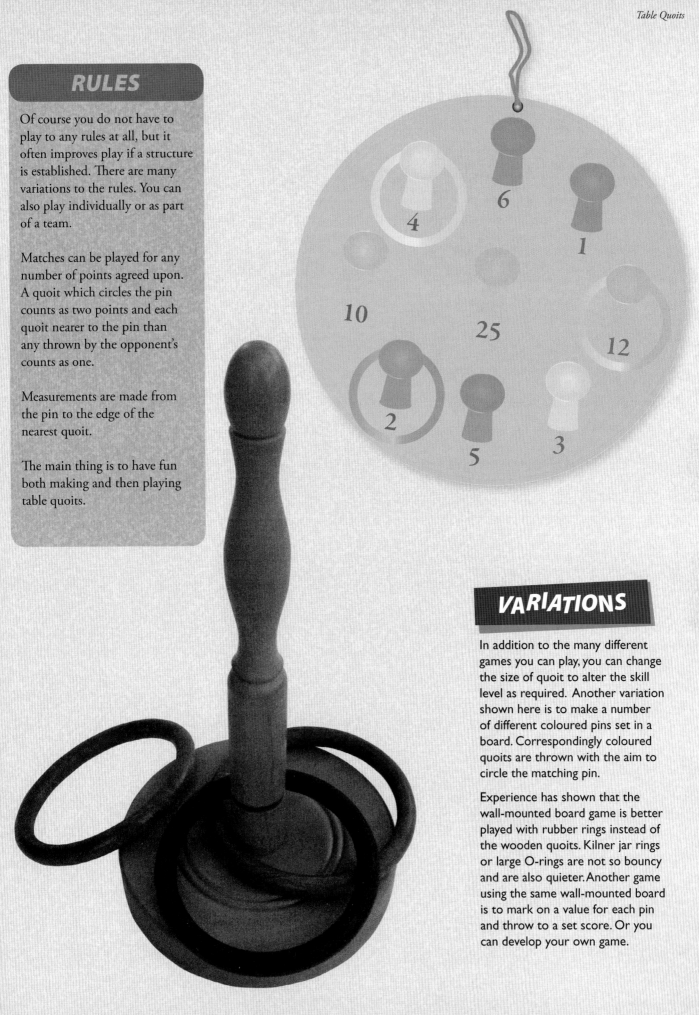

RULES

Of course you do not have to play to any rules at all, but it often improves play if a structure is established. There are many variations to the rules. You can also play individually or as part of a team.

Matches can be played for any number of points agreed upon. A quoit which circles the pin counts as two points and each quoit nearer to the pin than any thrown by the opponent's counts as one.

Measurements are made from the pin to the edge of the nearest quoit.

The main thing is to have fun both making and then playing table quoits.

VARIATIONS

In addition to the many different games you can play, you can change the size of quoit to alter the skill level as required. Another variation shown here is to make a number of different coloured pins set in a board. Correspondingly coloured quoits are thrown with the aim to circle the matching pin.

Experience has shown that the wall-mounted board game is better played with rubber rings instead of the wooden quoits. Kilner jar rings or large O-rings are not so bouncy and are also quieter. Another game using the same wall-mounted board is to mark on a value for each pin and throw to a set score. Or you can develop your own game.

PECKING CHICKENS

The Pendulum toy, as this type of movement is known, pre-dated clockwork motors and provided a simple and effective method of giving a realistic action to the figures. There were many variations, ranging from the washerwoman stirring her laundry with a cat lapping milk from a bowl by her side to the violin player. The toy made here is ideal for the woodturner. The chicks do not need to be identical, so if copy turning is not your strong point don't worry. In fact, the toy looks better if there are minor variations giving each chick a character of its own.

Use well-seasoned timber, the choice of which is entirely yours. I chose pau amarello (*Euxylophora paraensis*) for the chick's bodies and heads with rosita for the beaks, based on the colour of the natural wood. I have listed the species for reference only.

Cutting List

PLATFORM
1 piece $5^{29}/_{32}$in x $5^{29}/_{32}$in x $^{23}/_{32}$in (150mm x 150mm x 18mm) thick basswood (*Tilia americana*)

HANDLE
1 piece $^{29}/_{32}$in x $^{29}/_{32}$in x $5^{1}/_{2}$in (23mm x 23mm x 140) long sapele (*Entandrophragma cylindricum*)

BUSH
5 pieces $1^{1}/_{32}$in x $1^{1}/_{32}$in x $^{13}/_{16}$in (26mm x 26mm x 21mm) long beech (*Fagus sylvatica*)

LEG
5 pieces $^{5}/_{16}$in x $^{5}/_{16}$in x $1^{3}/_{8}$in (8mm x 8mm x 35mm) long beech (*Fagus sylvatica*)

BODY
1 piece $1^{1}/_{32}$in x $1^{1}/_{32}$in x $9^{1}/_{2}$in (26mm x 26mm x 240mm) long pau amarello (*Euxylophora paraensis*) (Makes 5)

HEAD
5 pieces $^{23}/_{32}$in x $^{23}/_{32}$in x $^{23}/_{32}$in (18mm x 18mm x 18mm) pau amarello (*Euxylophora paraensis*)

BEAK
1 piece $^{1}/_{4}$in x $^{1}/_{4}$in x $2^{15}/_{16}$in (6mm x 6mm x 75mm) long rosita (*Sickingia salvadorensis*) (Makes 5)

SPACER
2 pieces $^{5}/_{16}$in x $^{5}/_{16}$in x $1^{3}/_{8}$in (8mm x 8mm x 35mm) long beech (*Fagus sylvatica*) (Makes 10)

PENDULUM
1 piece $1^{1}/_{2}$in x $1^{1}/_{2}$in x $3^{1}/_{2}$in (38mm x 38mm x 90mm) long ash (*Fraxinus excelsior*)

In addition, you will need a $^{3}/_{32}$in ($2^{1}/_{2}$mm) diameter x $4^{11}/_{32}$in (110mm) long steel or brass rod, five $^{1}/_{4}$in (6mm) diameter x $1^{3}/_{16}$in (30mm) long dowels, a piece of thin red leather, $^{19}/_{32}$in (15mm) x $2^{11}/_{32}$in (60mm) will make five combs and 40in (1m) of strong twine. No.4 polyester whipping twine is ideal.

The finishing is all done on the lathe. It consists of an acrylic sanding sealer followed by two coats of melamine.

ANATOMY OF PECKING CHICKENS

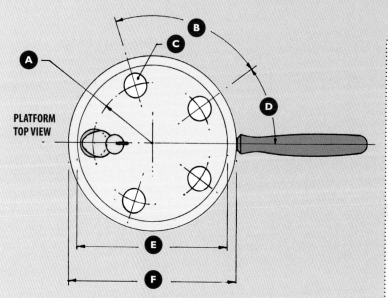

PLATFORM TOP VIEW

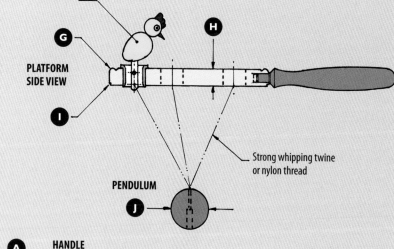

See chicken assembly drawing

PLATFORM SIDE VIEW

Strong whipping twine or nylon thread

PENDULUM

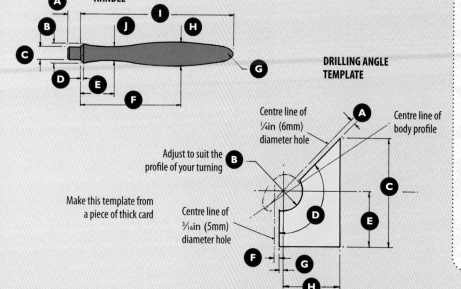

HANDLE

DRILLING ANGLE TEMPLATE

Centre line of ¼in (6mm) diameter hole

Centre line of body profile

Adjust to suit the profile of your turning

Make this template from a piece of thick card

Centre line of ³⁄₁₆in (5mm) diameter hole

PLATFORM

A 1³¹⁄₃₂in (50mm) radius

B 72°

C Drill 5 holes ¾in (20mm) diameter

D 36°

E 5¼in (133mm) diameter

F 5²³⁄₃₂in (145mm) diameter

G ¼in (6mm) bead

H ¹⁹⁄₃₂in (15mm)

I ³⁄₆₄in (1mm) square rebate

PENDULUM

J 1³⁄₈in (35mm) diameter

HANDLE

A ¹¹⁄₃₂in (9mm)

B ¹⁹⁄₃₂in (15mm) diameter

C ³⁄₈in (10mm) diameter

D ⁵⁄₆₄in (2mm)

E ²⁵⁄₃₂in (20mm)

F 3¹¹⁄₃₂in (85mm)

G ³⁄₁₆in (5mm) radius

H ²⁵⁄₃₂in (20mm) diameter

I 4¹¹⁄₃₂in (110mm)

J ¹⁵⁄₃₂in (12mm) diameter

DRILLING ANGLE TEMPLATE

A ⅛in (3mm)

B ½in (12mm) radius

C 2²⁷⁄₃₂in (72mm)

D 135°

E 1¹³⁄₃₂in (36mm)

F ⅛in (3mm)

G ⅛in (3mm)

H ²¹⁄₃₂in (42mm)

CHICKEN ASSEMBLY

Chicken must be free to pivot on the pin

Centre line of body profile

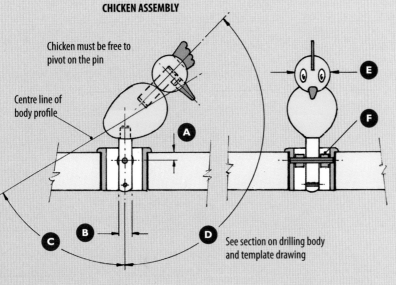

See section on drilling body and template drawing

BODY

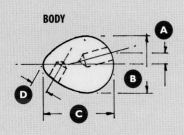

BUSH

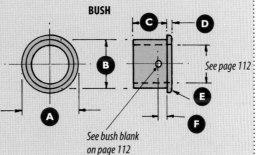

See page 112

See bush blank on page 112

LEG

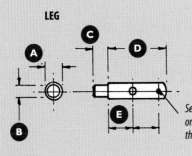

See leg blank on page 113 for these holes

BEAK

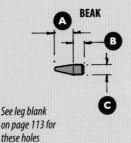

COMB

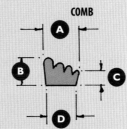

BUSH

- **A** $^{15}/_{16}$in (24mm) diameter
- **B** $^{3}/_{4}$in (20mm) diameter
- **C** $^{19}/_{32}$in (15mm)
- **D** $^{5}/_{64}$in (2mm)
- **E** $^{5}/_{64}$in (2mm) radius
- **F** $^{5}/_{32}$in (4mm)

LEG

- **A** $^{1}/_{4}$in (6mm) diameter
- **B** $^{3}/_{16}$in (5mm) diameter
- **C** $^{3}/_{16}$in (5mm)
- **D** $^{29}/_{32}$in (23mm)
- **E** $^{13}/_{32}$in (10mm)

BEAK

- **A** $^{5}/_{16}$in (8mm)
- **B** $^{5}/_{32}$in (4mm)
- **C** $^{5}/_{32}$in (4mm) diameter

COMB

- **A** $^{19}/_{32}$in (15mm)
- **B** $^{13}/_{32}$in (10mm)
- **C** $^{3}/_{16}$in (5mm)
- **D** $^{15}/_{32}$in (12mm)

CHICKEN ASSEMBLY

- **A** $^{5}/_{32}$in (4mm)
- **B** $^{1}/_{4}$in (6mm) diameter
- **C** 60°
- **D** 135°
- **E** $^{5}/_{8}$in (16mm) diameter
- **F** 2 x spacers $^{1}/_{4}$in (6mm) diameter x $^{5}/_{32}$in (4mm) wide

BODY

- **A** $^{1}/_{4}$in (6mm)
- **B** $^{15}/_{16}$in (24mm) diameter
- **C** $1^{3}/_{16}$in (30mm)
- **D** $^{11}/_{32}$in (9mm)

PLATFORM

1 Mark out the centre of the blank (see the anatomy drawing) and the position of the holes. Drill five ¾in (20mm) diameter holes through the blank **1**.

2 Cut off the corners with the band saw and mount on a glue chuck. Use the tailstock point to align the centre **2**.

3 Turn a ⅛in (3mm) deep dovetail recess to suit your own expansion chuck **3**. Use a scraper to true up the face of the blank. This will be the underside of the platform and will finish up being completely flat. The finish at this stage can be quite rough as we return to it later on.

4 Remove the blank from the glue chuck and remount, using the dovetail, onto the jaws of your expansion chuck. True up the outside edge to a diameter of 5²³⁄₃₂in (145mm) **4**.

5 Square up the face of the disc with a shear scraper and form the ¼in (6mm) bead decoration **5**.

6 Apply sanding sealer to the face and edge of the blank. When it's dry, finish with two coats of melamine.

7 Reverse mount the blank in a jam fit chuck or cole jaws if you have some. Make sure to protect the finish and face off the bottom of the blank to remove the dovetail and leave a flat surface. This will leave a finished thickness of ⅝in (15mm). Cut a ¹⁄₁₆in (1mm) square rebate on the edge. Sand, seal and finish as required then remove from the lathe **6**.

8 Drill a ⅜in (10mm) diameter x ⁷⁄₁₆in (11mm) deep hole at right angles to the edge to accommodate the spigot of the handle **7**.

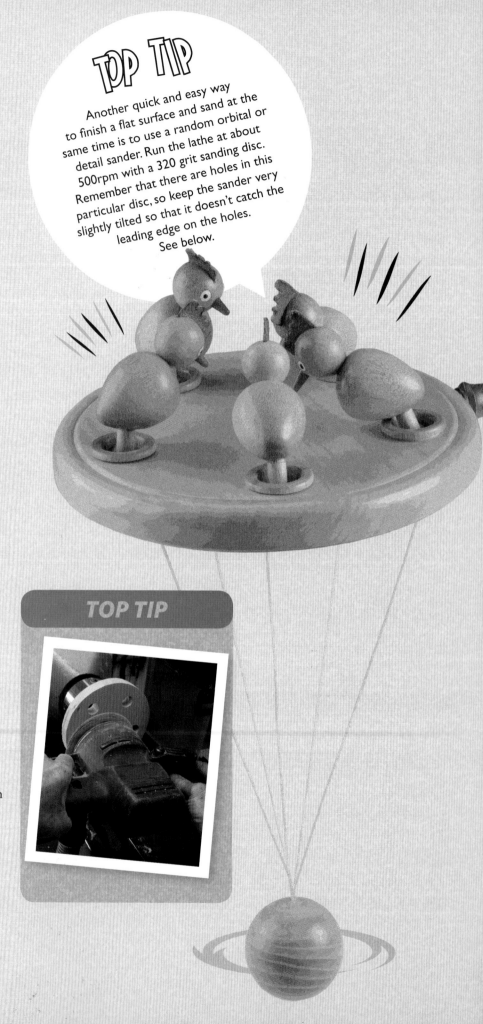

TOP TIP

Another quick and easy way to finish a flat surface and sand at the same time is to use a random orbital or detail sander. Run the lathe at about 500rpm with a 320 grit sanding disc. Remember that there are holes in this particular disc, so keep the sander very slightly tilted so that it doesn't catch the leading edge on the holes. See below.

TOP TIP

110

PLATFORM

HANDLE

1 Mark the diagonals at each end and mount the blank between centres. Rough down to a diameter of ²⁵⁄₃₂in (20mm) and cut a ³⁄₈in (10mm) diameter x ¹¹⁄₃₂in (9mm) long spigot at the tailstock end.

2 Form the profile with a spindle gouge, sand, seal and finish before reducing the waste to as small as safely possible and removing from the lathe. Cut off the waste, sand and finish the end profile.

HANDLE

BUSH

TOP TIP

Use a G-cramp to hold small, square blanks for this type of drilling operation.

BUSH BLANK

- **A** ½in (13mm)
- **B** ¹³⁄₁₆in (21mm)
- **C** ⁵⁄₁₆in (8mm)
- **D** 1in (26mm)
- **E** 1in (26mm)

BUSH (five required)

1 Mark and drill the blank as shown in the diagram **1**.

2 Turn a ⅝in (15mm) diameter spigot chuck to hold the pre-drilled blank and rough down to a ¹⁵⁄₁₆in (24mm) diameter **2a**. See the detail drawing on page 109. Square up the top and turn the ¾in (20mm) diameter body. Check the fit in the platform. This only needs to be a light push fit as it will be glued into the platform later on **2b**.

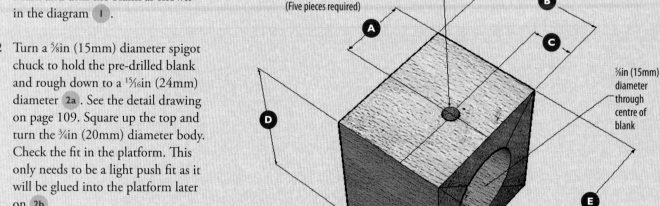

BUSH BLANK
(Five pieces required)

³⁄₃₂in (2.5mm) diameter or to suit diameter of your pin

⅝in (15mm) diameter through centre of blank

LEG (five required)

1 Mark and drill the blank as detailed in the drawing **1**.

2 Mount the blank between centres and turn the profile according to the detail drawing on page 109. Sand, seal and finish **2**.

3 Re-mount the blank in a 3-jaw chuck to form a slightly domed end on the bottom of the leg. Seal and finish the end to match the rest of the turning **3**.

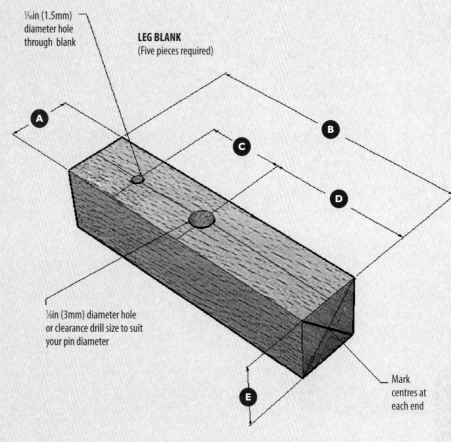

¹⁄₁₆in (1.5mm) diameter hole through blank

LEG BLANK
(Five pieces required)

Ⓐ Ⓑ Ⓒ Ⓓ

¹⁄₈in (3mm) diameter hole or clearance drill size to suit your pin diameter

Ⓔ

Mark centres at each end

LEG BLANK

- Ⓐ ⁵⁄₁₆in (8mm)
- Ⓑ 1³⁄₈in (35mm)
- Ⓒ ¹³⁄₃₂in (10mm) centres
- Ⓓ ²³⁄₃₂in (18mm)
- Ⓔ ⁵⁄₁₆in (8mm)

LEG

1

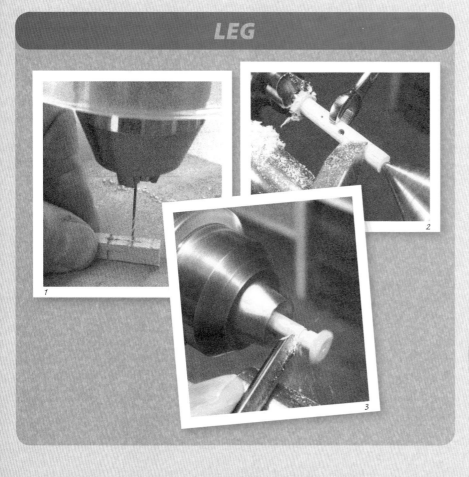

2

3

TOP TIP

Use a spanner to gauge the diameter as an easy alternative to setting up a pair of callipers.

BODY

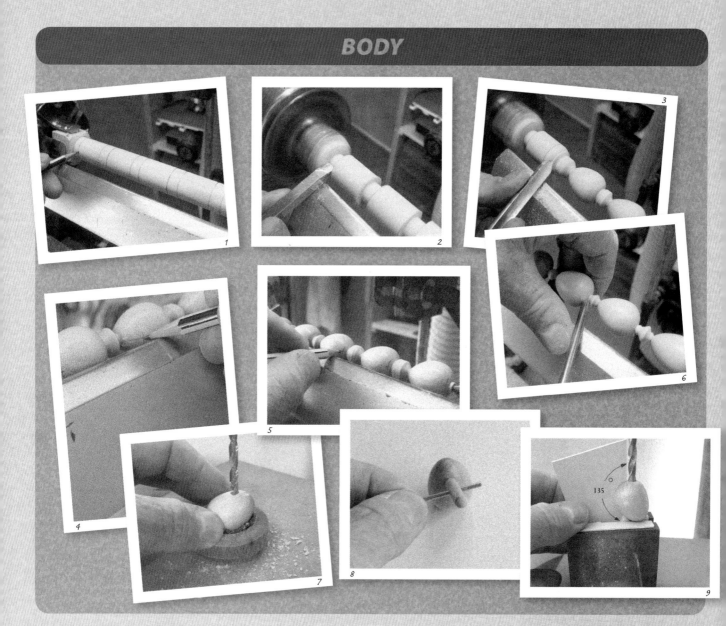

BODY (five required)

All five bodies are turned from the same blank.

1 Mount the blank directly into the jaws of a suitable compression chuck and rough down to a $^{31}\!/_{32}$in (25mm) diameter cylinder. Mark out five $1^{3}\!/_{16}$in (30mm) long sections, leaving approxiamately $^{13}\!/_{32}$in (10mm) between each ❶.

2 Use a parting tool to block out the bodies. Don't cut in too far at this stage, leave a minimum diameter of about $^{19}\!/_{32}$in (15mm) ❷.

3 Start to form the profiles, using a sharp spindle gouge working from the tailstock end. You can see all the profiles together which helps to compare shapes ❸.

4 When you are happy with the profiles, reduce the waste diameter further to allow you to sand gently if necessary. Seal and finish.

5 Lock the drive and, using the tool rest as a guide, mark a line $^{11}\!/_{32}$in (9mm) from the pointed end on the axis line. Use a compass to help gauge where the end point will be. See the drawing on page 109. Mark the other four profiles ❹.

6 Rotate the spindle through 180° and make another little mark ¼in (6mm) from the centre of the fat end of the body **5** .

7 Further reduce the waste to as small as safely possible. Support the turning to reduce vibration or premature breakage **6** . If you are not comfortable using this method, consider turning each body profile from an individual blank. Always work within your comfort zone.

8 Remove the spindle from the lathe and cut off the waste to give five bodies. Sand, seal and finish the profiles by hand as necessary.

9 Hold each body in a cup shaped jig with the pointed end up most and drill a ³⁄₁₆in (5mm) diameter hole x ¼in (6mm) deep in the centre of the mark. Ensure the drill enters at right angles to the profile surface. This should be at about 60° to the axis of the body **7** .

10 Glue the five legs into the bodies. Use a pin in the leg to ensure that the axes of the body and pin are set at 90° to each other **8** .

11 Hold the assembly in a small vice as shown and use the template to align the drilling angle. Drill a ¼in (6mm) diameter x ¹³⁄₃₂in (10mm) deep hole on the other mark made earlier. Again, drill at a right angle to the profile surface. Note the use of card on the cheeks of the vice to protect the finish **9** .

HEAD (five required)

1 Mark and drill the blank as shown in the drawing below.

2 Glue in the ¼in (6mm) x 1³⁄₁₆in (30mm) long dowel. When it is dry mount in a 3-jaw chuck on the lathe **1** .

3 Rough the blank down to a ⁵⁄₈in (16mm) diameter cylinder and mark a line on the centre line of the ⁵⁄₃₂in (4mm) diameter hole. True up the ends to ⁵⁄₁₆in (8mm) each side of the line **2** .

4 Turn the spherical shape equally around the centre line using a small spindle gouge. Be careful not to cut into the dowel. Sand, seal and finish before removing from the lathe **3** . Do not assemble the head to the body at this stage.

HEAD

Drill ¼in (6mm) diameter x ¹³⁄₃₂in (10mm) deep in centre of blank

HEAD BLANK
(Five pieces required)

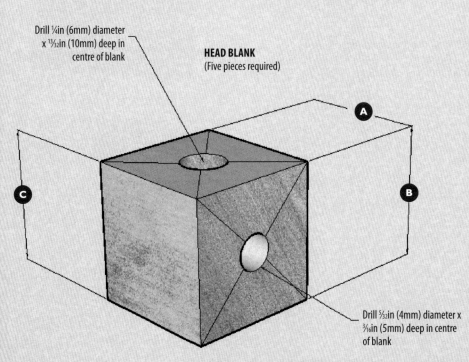

Drill ⁵⁄₃₂in (4mm) diameter x ³⁄₁₆in (5mm) deep in centre of blank

HEAD BLANK

A ²³⁄₃₂in (18mm)
B ²³⁄₃₂in (18mm)
C ²³⁄₃₂in (18mm)

BEAK (five required)

All the beaks are turned from the same blank.

1 Mark the centres at each end and mount on the lathe between centres to rough down to a ⁵⁄₃₂in (4mm) diameter dowel ❶.

2 Remount the dowel in a 3-jaw chuck with sufficient length exposed to form each beak ❷. Sand, seal and finish each one before parting off. Do not make the beaks too sharp. (See the drawing on page 109.)

BEAK

TOP TIP

Most roughing gouges are fairly large and a bit clumsy for this small-scale stuff. Use a ³⁄₈in (10mm) bowl gouge instead of the usual roughing down tool.

SPACER

SPACER (ten required)

1 Drill a ³⁄₃₂in (2½mm) diameter hole vertically through the centre of each blank. Drill carefully and in little bites to prevent the drill from wandering off centre ❶.

2 Mount between centres and rough down to a ¼in (6mm) diameter.

3 Re-mount in a 3-jaw chuck. Sand, seal and finish before parting off ¹⁵⁄₃₂in (4mm) long sections to make ten spacers ❷. Use a length of wire to catch each spacer as it parts company with the lathe.

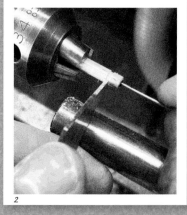

COMB (five required)

1 Draw the profiles of all five combs onto the piece of red leather then cut them out using a small pair of scissors.

PENDULUM

COMB

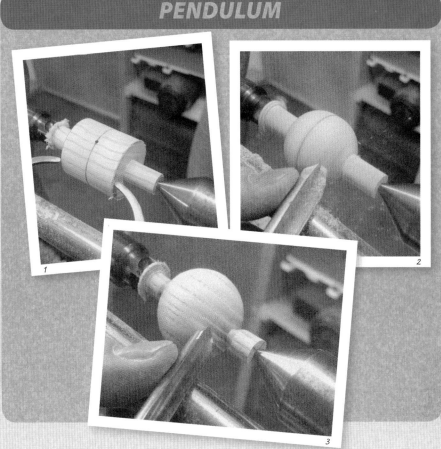

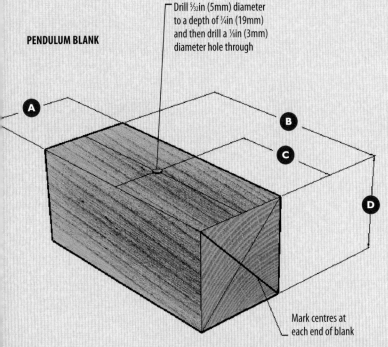

PENDULUM BLANK

A 1½in (38mm) **C** 1¾in (45mm)

B 3½in (90mm) **D** 1½in (38mm)

PENDULUM

1 Mark and drill the blank as shown in the drawing below.

2 Mount between centres and turn down to a 1⅜in (35mm) diameter cylinder. Mark a line around the middle, passing through the centre of the holes. Cut ¹³⁄₃₂in (10mm) diameter spigots at each end to leave a 1⅜in (35mm) diameter x 1⅜in (35mm) long blank with the line around the centre ①.

3 Use a spindle gouge to cut in each side of the centre line to form the sphere ②. Use the sphere turning jig if necessary to form the perfect sphere. This pendulum does not have to be in the shape of a sphere. It will work just as well as an egg shape, cylinder or disc.

4 Continue to form the profile, reducing the waste diameter to as small as safely possible as you go ③. Sand, seal and apply the finish. Remove from the lathe. Cut off the waste using a sharp blade and sand in the profile before sealing and finishing these little areas by hand.

PENDULUM BLANK

Drill ⁵⁄₃₂in (5mm) diameter to a depth of ¾in (19mm) and then drill a ⅛in (3mm) diameter hole through

Mark centres at each end of blank

PIVOT PINS

1 First cut the rod into five ¾in (20mm) lengths.

CHICKEN ASSEMBLY

1 Mount the head in a bench vice and saw a kerf line in the top, in line with the beak. The saw kerf should match the thickness and length of the leather comb, see the drawing on page 109. Cut the exposed length of dowel down to ⁵⁄₁₆in (8mm) to fit the hole in the body **1** .

2 Glue the combs onto the heads, then glue the heads into the five bodies.

3 Glue in the beaks and paint the eyes.

4 Cut the twine into five equal lengths then thread a length through the bottom leg hole. Tie a knot in this twine to prevent it pulling back out. Trim off the excess as necessary **2** .

5 Push a pin into the hole in the side of the bush and thread on a spacer, followed by the leg and another spacer. You may need small pliers or tweezers here. Push the pin through

the other wall of the bush. Hold the bush and the chicken in an upright position and check that the chicken will fall forwards with its head down. This movement must be very free

and not binding on the pivot pin. Make any adjustment necessary. The pin does not need to be glued as it will be trapped when the bush is fitted in the platform.

CHICKEN ASSEMBLY

6 Glue the handle into the platform and glue in the five bushes. Make sure the chicken/bush assemblies are arranged to face the centre and that, with all heads down, they are equally spaced.

7 Gather the strings together and thread them through the ⅛in (3mm) hole in the pendulum and out the other side.

8 Tie an overhand knot loosely in the bunch of twine about 7in (175mm) from the platform. Holding the whole assembly by the knot or pendulum, check that the platform lies horizontally with all the strings equally taut. Adjust as necessary before pulling the knot tight and trimming the ends **3** .

9 Pull the knot into the large hole in the pendulum to tidy everything up. The chickens are ready to be fed.

How it Works

Hold the toy in front of you by the handle. The chickens will fall forward with their heads pulled down by gravity. But the pendulum will pull each chick back to the upright position as the player gently swirls the platform to make the pendulum swing in a circular motion. This simulates the pecking action of the chickens as they eat seeds from the ground.

This toy is a development of the stacking discs on page 52. It is ideal for slightly older children who are able to work out where each piece goes. The finished item also looks nice on a nursery shelf rather than tucked away in a toy box.

STACKING FIGURE

This is a good project to paint with some bright colours, so you can use up scrap pieces of different timbers. The character and style of the toy can be changed significantly by using alternative colours to the ones shown here.

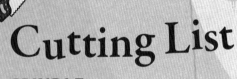

Cutting List

SPINDLE

1 piece $^{23}/_{32}$in x $^{23}/_{32}$in x $9\frac{1}{2}$in
(18mm x 18mm x 240mm) long

LOWER LEGS

1 piece $1^{31}/_{32}$in x $1^{31}/_{32}$in x $1^{25}/_{32}$in
(50mm x 50mm x 45mm) long

UPPER LEGS

1 piece $1^{31}/_{32}$in x $1^{31}/_{32}$in x $1^{25}/_{32}$in
(50mm x 50mm x 45mm) long

BELT

1 piece $1^{31}/_{32}$in x $1^{31}/_{32}$in x $^{15}/_{32}$in
(50mm x 50mm x 12mm) long

LOWER BODY

1 piece $2\frac{1}{4}$in x $2\frac{1}{4}$in x $1^{25}/_{32}$in
(58mm x 58mm x 45mm) long

UPPER BODY

1 piece $2\frac{1}{4}$ x $1^{31}/_{32}$in x $1^{25}/_{32}$in
(58mm x 50mm x 45mm) long
(See the drilling detail drawing on
page 124)

HEAD

1 piece $1^{21}/_{32}$in x $1^{21}/_{32}$in x $1^{3}/_{16}$in
(42mm x 42mm x 30mm) long

HAT

1 piece $1^{31}/_{32}$in x $1^{31}/_{32}$in x $2\frac{1}{8}$in
(50mm x 50mm x 54mm) long

ARMS

2 pieces $^{3}/_{4}$in x $^{3}/_{8}$in x $2\frac{3}{4}$in
(20mm x 10mm x 70mm) long
(See the assembly/drilling detail
on page 125)

BASE

1 piece $3\frac{1}{16}$in x $3\frac{1}{16}$in x $1\frac{3}{16}$in
(78mm x 78mm x 30mm) thick

**In addition to the above, you will
need two No.6 gauge countersunk
woodscrews x $^{3}/_{4}$in (19mm) long to
fit the arms to the body.**

ANATOMY OF A STACKING SOLDIER

SOLDIER

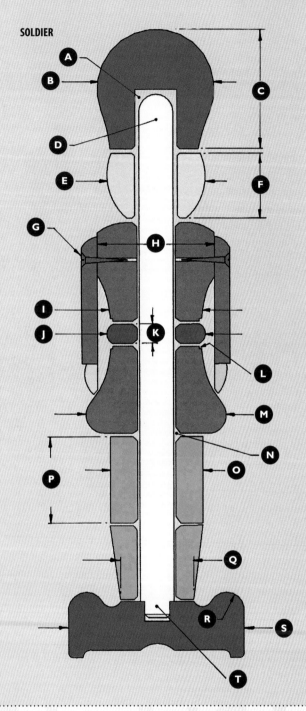

SOLDIER

A ⅝in (16mm) diameter x 1³⁄₁₆in (30mm) long

B 1⁷⁄₈in (48mm) diameter

C 1³¹⁄₃₂in (50mm)

D ⁹⁄₁₆in (15mm) diameter x 9⅛in (232mm) long

E 1⁹⁄₁₆in (40mm) diameter

F 1³⁄₃₂in (28mm)

G 2 x No.6 countersunk woodscrews

H 1³¹⁄₃₂in (50mm) across flats

I 1¹³⁄₁₆in (46mm) diameter

J 1⁷⁄₈in (48mm) diameter

K ¹³⁄₃₂in (10mm)

L ³⁄₆₄in (1mm) square rebates

M 2³⁄₁₆in (56mm) diameter

N ⁵⁄₆₄in (2mm) x 45° chamfers

O 1¹³⁄₁₆in (46mm) diameter

P 1⁹⁄₁₆in (40mm) typical length of body part

Q 1¹³⁄₃₂in (36mm) diameter

R ¼in (6mm) radius

S 3in (76mm) diameter

T ½in (12mm) diameter x ¹¹⁄₃₂in (9mm) long spigot

ARM

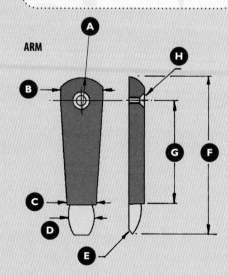

ARM

A ¹⁹⁄₃₂in (15mm) radius

B ²³⁄₃₂in (18mm) diameter

C ⁹⁄₁₆in (14mm) diameter

D ¹⁵⁄₃₂in (12mm) diameter

E Sand profile inside to match body

F 2⁹⁄₁₆in (65mm)

G 1²⁵⁄₃₂in (45mm)

H Clearance hole countersunk to suit screws

SPINDLE

1 Mark the centres on each end of the blank and mount between centres. Rough down to a diameter of about ⅝in (16mm), just removing the flat surfaces. Use a skew chisel to plane down the spindle to a finished diameter of ⁹⁄₁₆in (15mm).

2 Form a radius at the tailstock end, leaving sufficient waste to hold the blank for sanding.

3 Measure the length required from the top of the spindle to the end and form a ½in (12mm) diameter x ¹¹⁄₃₂in (9mm) long spigot at the headstock end. In the example shown here, the length of spindle is 4 x 1⁹⁄₁₆in (40mm) (body and legs) + ¹³⁄₃₂in (10mm) (belt) + 1³⁄₃₂in (28mm) (head) + ³¹⁄₃₂in (25mm) (hat) + ¹¹⁄₃₂in (9mm) (spigot). Making a total length of 9⅛in (232mm).

4 Sand and seal the spindle before parting off from the lathe. Sand in the top profile by hand after cutting off the waste.

SPINDLE

HAT

HAT (first stage)

1 Mark the centres on each end of the blank and drill a ⅝in (16mm) diameter hole into the end grain x 1³⁄₁₆in (30mm) deep.

2 Mount between centres with the tailstock centre in the hole that you have just drilled and rough down to a cylinder, just removing any flat surfaces. Turn a dovetail spigot at the headstock end to suit your compression chuck **1** .

3 Re-mount the blank in the compression jaws and square up the end grain **2a** . Turn a ⁵⁄₆₄in (2mm) x 45° chamfer around the hole. This will provide an enlarged lead in diameter, making the toy easier to use. This chamfer will be repeated on all the pieces top and bottom. Sand and seal the end grain before removing the blank to finish later. Before starting to turn the legs, body, belt, head and finishing the hat, you may find it helpful to make the mandrel chuck shown here.

This is used to hold all the body parts. It can be made from any scrap piece of timber and will more than repay the time taken to make **2b** .

MANDREL CHUCK

A Dovetail spigot to match your own chuck

B 1³¹⁄₃₂in (50mm) diameter x ¹³⁄₃₂in (10mm)

C 1³⁄₁₆in (30mm) diameter x ³⁄₁₆in (5mm)

D ⅝in (16mm) diameter x ³¹⁄₃₂in (25mm) long

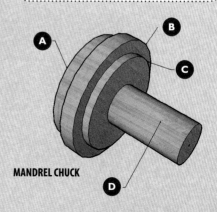

MANDREL CHUCK

123

LEGS (two blanks)

1 Mark the diagonals on one end of each blank (end grain) and drill a ⅝in (16mm) diameter hole through each. Again, use proper support to hold the blank while drilling **1**.

2 Mount one blank onto the spigot chuck and bring up the tailstock into the hole in the blank. It should be a reasonably tight fit on the spigot, but will get extra support from a standard 60° live centre.

3 Form the profile of the leg as necessary **2** (see anatomy drawing). Cut the blank to length, using the long point of your skew, and soften the corners and edges. Withdraw the tailstock and turn a ⁵⁄₆₄in (2mm) lead in chamfer around the ⅝in (16mm) hole. Sand and seal before reverse mounting the blank to complete the other end **3**.

4 Now repeat steps 2 and 3 for the upper leg.

BODY (two blanks)

1 Mark the diagonals on the two body blanks and drill a ⅝in (16mm) diameter hole through each.

2 Mark the upper body blank in accordance with the dimensions shown below. Drill a pilot hole of ⁵⁄₆₄in (2mm) diameter for the arm screws through the 1³¹⁄₃₂in (50mm) width of the blank **1**.

3 Mount the body blanks on the mandrel and turn the profiles as required. In the case of the upper body, this will leave small flats each side for the arms **2**.

4 Make certain to form the lead in chamfers around the central hole at each end and to soften all sharp edges. Sand and seal all surfaces.

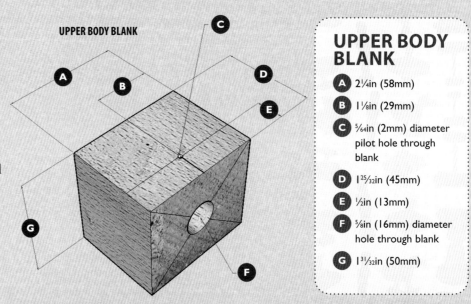

UPPER BODY BLANK

UPPER BODY BLANK

A 2¼in (58mm)

B 1⅛in (29mm)

C ⁵⁄₆₄in (2mm) diameter pilot hole through blank

D 1²⁵⁄₃₂in (45mm)

E ½in (13mm)

F ⅝in (16mm) diameter hole through blank

G 1³¹⁄₃₂in (50mm)

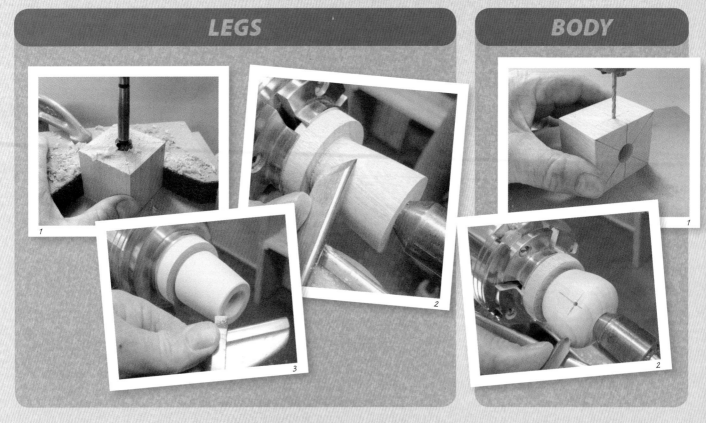

LEGS

BODY

BELT

HEAD

HAT

BELT

1 Mark the centre of the blank and drill a ⅝in (16mm) diameter hole through it.

2 Mount the blank on the spigot and rough down to a cylinder. Use one of the body or leg parts to help support the belt on the spigot chuck.

3 Finish off the profile with a small spindle gouge, remembering to soften the edges and also to cut the chamfers both sides.

4 Sand and seal as necessary.

HEAD

1 Mark the centre in one end grain face of the head blank and drill a ⅝in (16mm) diameter hole through the blank.

2 Mount on the spigot and form the profile of the head. Then sand and seal.

HAT (finish)

1 Mount the part turned blank on the spigot and bring up the tailstock. Finish turning the profile. Sand and seal.

Remove the spigot chuck and keep it safely to one side to use for the base turning. Alignment will not be a problem because the diameter of the spigot, when re-mounted, is reduced.

ARMS

The arms are made from a composite of the two pieces shown in the cutting list. Apply some adhesive to each mating face. Place a sheet of newspaper between the joint, clamp the blanks together and leave to dry.

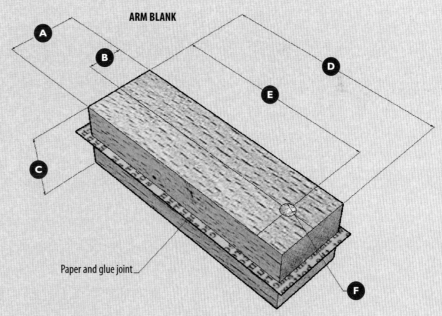

ARM BLANK

A **B** **D** **E** **C** **F**

Paper and glue joint

ARM BLANK

A ¾in (20mm)

B ⅜in (10mm)

C ¾in (20mm)

D 2¾in (70mm)

E 2⁷⁄₁₆in (62mm)

F ⁵⁄₃₂in (3.5mm) diameter hole through blank

1 When the assembly is dry, mark the diagonals on each end of the composite blank. To ensure that both arms are identical, the centre point must fall on the joint line.

2 Drill a clearance hole for the No.6 screws through the blank as detailed in the drawing on page 125 ①.

3 Mount the blank between centres.

4 Turn the arm and hand profile as shown in the anatomy drawing ②.

5 Sand and seal the turning then part off from the lathe. Split open the two halves using a thin blade ③. Clean off the paper inside the arms and soften the sharp edges. Sand and seal the inside faces.

6 Use a countersink bit in your drill stand to sink the holes for the screw heads ④.

TOP TIP

It is very important when turning split (glued together) blanks, not to apply too much pressure at the joint line and open up the glue join. If you do not possess a ring or cup centre for your tailstock, a simple remedy is to pop an olive fitting over the point on your live centre. This will prevent the point from forcing the join open ②. These fittings are used in plumbing and are available from DIY outlets.

ARMS

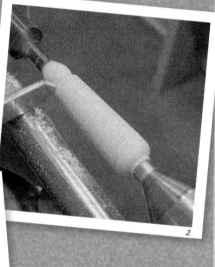

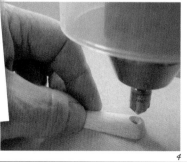

BASE

1 Mark the diagonals on one face of the blank and scribe a 1¹⁷⁄₃₂in (39mm) radius around the blank. Drill a 2in (50mm) diameter x ³⁄₁₆in (5mm) deep recess in the centre. Use a well-supported blank to avoid the possibility of the drill bit picking up and spinning the blank out of your grip, potentially causing serious injury ①.

2 Cut out the circle on the band saw, following the previously drawn pencil line ②.

3 Mount the blank on an expanding chuck and form the top of the base profile (see anatomy drawing) ③.

4 Insert a Jacobs-type chuck in the tailstock and drill a ½in (12mm) diameter x ¹³⁄₃₂in (10mm) deep hole for the spindle ④.

BASE

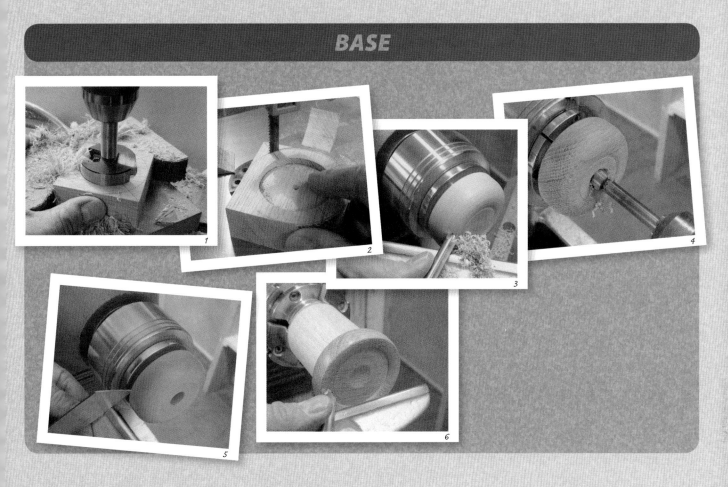

5 Square up the rear face using a parting tool and sand down to 320 grade if you are going to paint the toy. This will give a bit of key for the paint **5** .

6 Seal the surface with an acrylic sanding sealer.

7 Re-mount the ⅝in (16mm) spigot chuck into your compression chuck and reduce the diameter to ½in (12mm). Mount the base blank onto the spigot and refine the underside of the base. Ensure the bottom face is flat or slightly concave so it does not wobble in use **6** . Sand and seal this face then put to one side.

All the parts are now made and ready for painting. Keep the decoration simple and use bright colours as they will appeal to young children. I have used artist's acrylic paint and several coats of acrylic lacquer to finish.

ASSEMBLY

1 Glue the spindle to the base.

2 Screw the arms in position to the upper body. Make the joints loose enough to allow the arm to swing, but tight enough for the arm to remain in any position. You can apply a drop of thin cyanoacrylate glue into the holes inside the body to lock the screws if required.

VARIATIONS

Make a different hat to turn your stacking toy into a sailor, clown, policeman or anything else you wish. A fireman is always a popular figure, as shown here.

DIAVOLO

This is another toy whose origins trace back to the Orient. The game has been played in China for centuries where it is known as *Kouen-Gen*. The toy consists of two sticks joined together with a length of cord and a spinning top in the shape of a spool.

HISTORY

There are a number of popular names for this toy. Diavolo is recorded in use in England in 1470AD and comes from *di* meaning two parts and *avolo* meaning flight.

The popular name of diabolo was first applied at the beginning of the nineteenth century and was probably taken from the Greek word *diabollo*, meaning to throw. This seems very likely as one of the main actions of the game is to throw the spool between two or more players. Another meaning of the word *diabollo* is to slander, this also has some relevance as the Slanderer in Chief is thought to be the Devil. (*Diable* is devil in many languages). The toy was given the name Devil on Two Sticks around the same time, probably because of the difficulty in acquiring the skill needed to play.

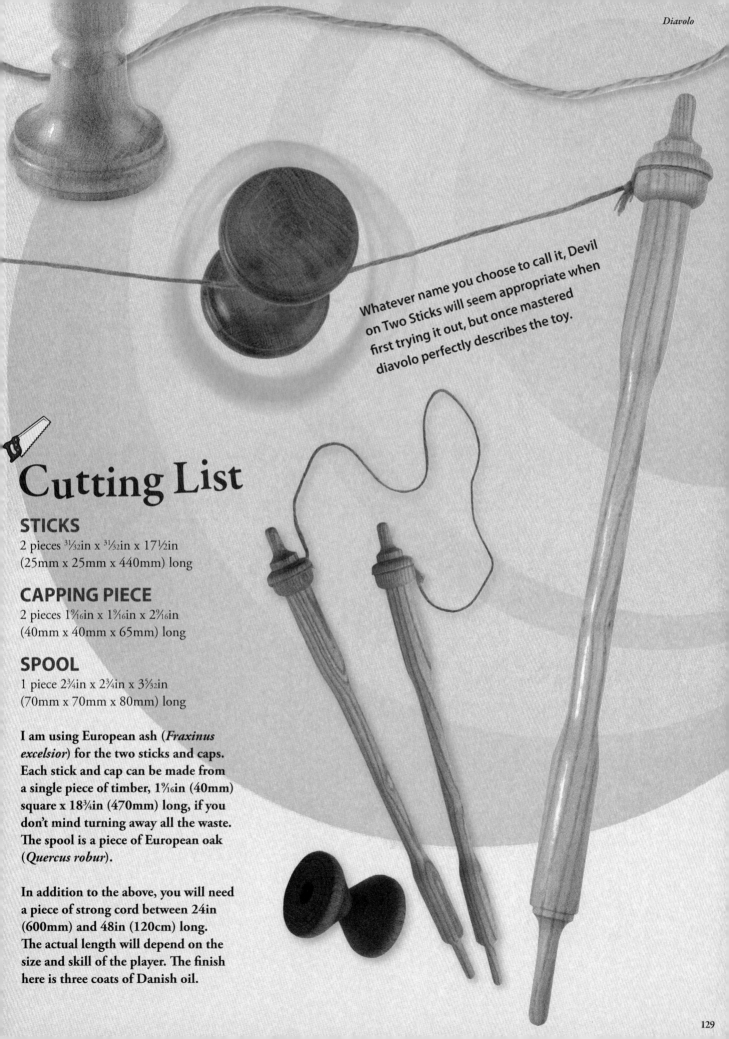

Whatever name you choose to call it, Devil on Two Sticks will seem appropriate when first trying it out, but once mastered diavolo perfectly describes the toy.

Cutting List

STICKS

2 pieces $^{31}/_{32}$in x $^{31}/_{32}$in x 17½in
(25mm x 25mm x 440mm) long

CAPPING PIECE

2 pieces 1$^9/_{16}$in x 1$^9/_{16}$in x 2$^9/_{16}$in
(40mm x 40mm x 65mm) long

SPOOL

1 piece 2¾in x 2¾in x 3$^5/_{32}$in
(70mm x 70mm x 80mm) long

I am using European ash (*Fraxinus excelsior*) for the two sticks and caps. Each stick and cap can be made from a single piece of timber, 1$^9/_{16}$in (40mm) square x 18¾in (470mm) long, if you don't mind turning away all the waste. The spool is a piece of European oak (*Quercus robur*).

In addition to the above, you will need a piece of strong cord between 24in (600mm) and 48in (120cm) long. The actual length will depend on the size and skill of the player. The finish here is three coats of Danish oil.

ANATOMY OF A DIAVOLO

CAPPING PIECE
(Two required)

Drill ⅞in (22mm) diameter x ³⁄₁₆in (5mm) deep, then ⅝in (16mm) diameter x ¹⁵⁄₃₂in (12mm) deep on the same centre

CAPPING PIECE

- **A** ¹⁵⁄₁₆in (24mm)
- **B** ¼in (6mm)
- **C** ¹³⁄₃₂in (10mm) diameter
- **D** 1¼in (32mm) diameter
- **E** ⅞in (22mm) diameter
- **F** ³⁄₁₆in (5mm) typical radius
- **G** ⁵⁄₆₄in (2mm) wide x 1³⁄₃₂in (28mm) diameter
- **H** ⁹⁄₁₆in (14mm)
- **I** 2⁵⁄₃₂in (55mm)
- **J** 1¹³⁄₃₂in (36mm)

STICKS

- **K** ⅝in (16mm) diameter x ¹³⁄₃₂in (10mm) long spigot
- **L** 3¹⁵⁄₁₆in (100mm)
- **M** ⅞in (22mm)
- **N** 16½in (420mm)
- **O** 6¾in (175mm)
- **P** ⅝in (16mm) diameter
- **Q** 2in (50mm)
- **R** ¹³⁄₃₂in (10mm) diameter

SPOOL

- **S** 2¹⁵⁄₁₆in (75mm)
- **T** 2⁵⁄₈in (67mm)
- **U** ⅞in (22mm) diameter

STICKS

SPOOL

See cap detail drawing

Gently blend the diameters together

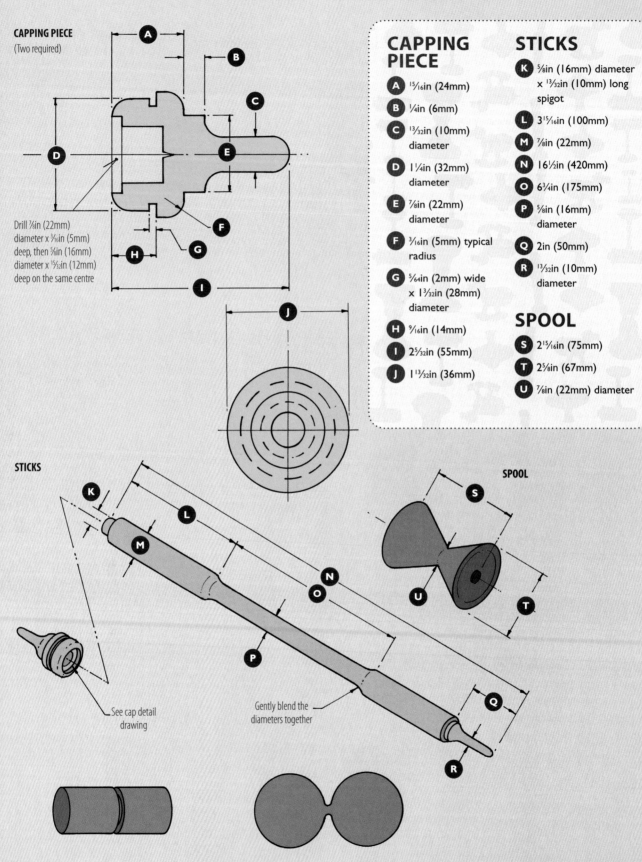

STICKS

1 Mark the centres at each end of the blanks and mount between centres on the lathe.

2 My tool rest is not long enough to cover the whole length of the turning, so I have worked in stages along the profile. I started work at the tailstock end and finished at the headstock **1**.

3 Rough the blank down to a ⅞in (22mm) diameter cylinder and turn the profile at the tailstock end as shown in the drawing on page 130. Leave ³⁄₁₆in (5mm) or so on the length to allow removal of the centre mark later **2**.

4 Reduce the diameter of the centre section to ⅝in (16mm) and blend the two diameters together **3**.

STICKS

5 Cut a ⅝in (16mm) diameter x ¹³⁄₃₂in (10mm) long spigot at the headstock end for the capping piece **4**.

6 Sand down to 400 grit abrasive and form a radius at the tailstock end sufficient to remove all trace of the centre mark **5**.

7 Remove from the lathe and cut off the waste pips at each end. Sand the end profile by hand if necessary.

8 Make the other stick in a similar fashion, using the first one as a guide **6**.

CAPPING PIECE

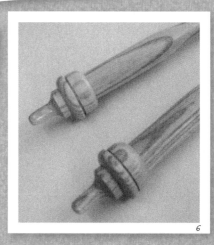

CAPPING PIECE

1 Mark the centre point on each end in the usual manner and drill a ⅞in (22mm) diameter x ³⁄₁₆in (5mm) deep hole vertically into one of the ends **1** .

2 Drill a second hole using the centre point as a guide to drill a ⅝in (16mm) diameter x ¹⁵⁄₃₂in (12mm) deep hole, see the detail drawing on page 130 **2** .

3 Mount the blank between centres with the tailstock in the holes you have just drilled and rough down to a 1½in (38mm) diameter cylinder **3** .

4 Refer to the drawing on page 130 and turn the profile. Use a narrow parting tool to cut a recess for the cord **4** .

5 Continue forming the profile using a spindle gouge then sand down to match the finish on the sticks. Reduce the waste to as small as safely possible before removing from the lathe **5** .

6 Cut off the waste pip with a sharp blade and sand in the profile. Make another end cap for the other stick.

7 Glue the caps onto the sticks using a good PVA-type adhesive. When dry, apply three coats of Danish oil **6** .

SPOOL

There are many ways of turning this shape. Just mounting the blank between centres would seem the most obvious and easy solution, but the finished profile may need some adjustment to its trim after the turning is removed from the lathe. The following method makes that operation relatively simple.

1 Mark the centres on each end of the blank and vertically drill a ⅝in (16mm) diameter x ²⁵⁄₃₂in (20mm) deep hole into the centre at each end **1** .

2 Make a ⅝in (16mm) spigot chuck from a piece of scrap timber. Fit the blank with the tailstock brought up into the hole at the other end **2** .

3 Rough down to a 2⅝in (67mm) diameter cylinder and square up the ends with a skew chisel to give an overall length of 2¹³⁄₁₆in (75mm). You may wish to add some decorative rings or beads to the end profiles. Do not make these too delicate as the whole top will take quite a bashing in its lifetime **3** .

4 Mark a line around the exact centre point and two more lines ¹³⁄₃₂in (10mm) from each end **4** .

5 Use a parting tool to undercut the diameter on the centre line and a gouge to form the cone shapes each side equally as you go **5** .

6 Use a pair of compass points to maintain the exact centre point. Shape the cone profiles from the pencil lines at each end to the centre **6** .

7 Reduce the diameter at the centre to ⅞in (22mm). Using a spindle gouge, round all the sharp corners and sand the blank down to 400 grit **7** . Mark the spigot and spool alignment then, leaving the spigot in place, remove the spool from the lathe.

SPOOL

1 2 3 4 5 6 7

TRIMMING THE TOP

It is not absolutely essential that the centre of gravity is exactly on the centre line that you have worked so hard to maintain. The wood may have variations of density along its length. However it will help the novice player considerably to start the top spinning if it balances about its midpoint.

To achieve this happy state, place the spool on a thin rod as shown and see if it will balance.

If it's way out of balance, you can remove some weight from the heavier side in one of two ways:

a) Remount the spool on the spigot chuck. Make sure you fit the same end to the spigot having marked it as above.

Trim off a little material from the heavier side. Repeat this procedure until the spool sits in equilibrium on the rod, or

b) Drill into the end hole at the heavy side with the ⅝in (16mm) drill bit to remove a little more wood.

Either of these methods will be effective, but should be carried out a little at a time. Otherwise you may find that you also need to remove some weight from the other side. To the seasoned player, a slight imbalance doesn't matter.

When you are happy with the finished turning, apply the finish of your choice. Here, I am oiling the spool to match the sticks. If you don't like the holes at each end, you can turn some small plugs.

ASSEMBLY

Tie the cord around the grooves in the capping pieces and you are ready to start playing.

HOW TO PLAY

For obvious reasons this toy is not suitable for indoor use, especially when learning. The toy is equally appropriate for individual amusement or for teams of two or more players.

Start with the top placed on the ground and the axis of the spool at right angles to the player. The cord passes underneath the central point. One stick must be lower than the other. Raising the lower stick rapidly lifts the top from the ground and will start it spinning, giving it a certain measure of stability. Repeat this whipping action to get the top spinning faster and faster on the cord. The faster it spins, the more stable it becomes. Don't get too ambitious, just master the art of getting the top to spin with its midpoint resting on the cord.

With practice the spinning top can be thrown upwards from the cord, then caught again on the cord. Firstly, reverse the height of the sticks, bringing the lower one to the higher position, and repeat the lift-rotation action to impart more spin and once again lift the top into the air.

The spool must be kept spinning in the same direction. Correct any slight imbalance in flight by catching it with your right hand moved towards you, if the spool tilts down toward the player. If it tilts away from you, move your left hand backwards, away from you. For left-handed players these movements are reversed.

The tricks include rotating the top on its cord; balancing the spinning top and making it appear to walk along one of the sticks; tossing the top to make it appear to climb the cord; and catching the rapidly spinning top on the crossed sticks, either facing downwards or at their tips. With some practice and a little dexterity, the top can be set spinning just by using the stick. The game can also be played without any sticks at all, with the cord being held in the player's hands.

For the serious player, a book entitled *Diabolo, the Game and its Tricks* written by David Ward in 1908, is recommended. It is probably out of print, but you may find it in a good reference library, a second-hand bookshop or on the Internet.

VARIATIONS

There are numerous variations, both to the shape of the top itself and to the method of play. The two cones joined at their apex is a good starting point, but the dumbbell and cylinder shapes shown on page 130 are slightly more difficult to use. You could also devise and make your own unique shape.

How it Works

Just as a normal top will not be able to stand upright while at rest, but appears to defy gravity and stand very steadily on its point when spinning, the diavolo top will also lack stability until it starts to spin.

The faster it rotates, the more stable it becomes. The difference between these two types of top is that the latter spins on its side, either supported on the cord or unsupported when it's thrown into the air.

MUSIC MAN

The pull-along toy is a real favourite of the very young and has been around for literally thousands of years. Simply pulling the toy creates the interesting and amusing actions of the character on board, from chickens flapping their wings and even laying eggs, to this little man playing the xylophone and turning his head as he goes along.

Cutting List

PLATFORM
7½in x 3⅜in x ⅜in
(190mm x 86mm x 10mm) thick
(Finished size)

AXLE BLOCK
(four required)
1³⁄₁₆in x 2⁹⁄₃₂in x ⅜in
(30mm x 23mm x 10mm) thick

XYLOPHONE BASE
2¾in x 2in x 2¹¹⁄₃₂in
(70mm x 50mm x 60mm) long

BODY
2¹⁄₃₂in x 2¹⁄₃₂in x 3¾in
(52mm x 52mm x 95mm) long

HAND
⅝in x ⅝in x 2¹⁵⁄₁₆in
(16mm x 16mm x 75mm) long
(Makes two)

Because the toy is for very young children, it should be kept fairly simple and robust. The project is a nice blend of non-turned items, between centre work and off centre turning. The timbers chosen will depend more on their natural colours than anything else. I am also going to paint the body, arms and wheels with bright colours.

The finish here will be sanding sealer to all surfaces, except those faces which are glued together. The finished item is then sprayed with a gloss melamine lacquer.

HEAD
1⁹⁄₁₆in x 1⁹⁄₁₆in x 1⁹⁄₁₆in
(40mm x 40mm x 40mm)

BUSH
⁷⁄₈in x ⁷⁄₈in x ²⁵⁄₃₂in
(22mm x 22mm x 20mm)

ARM (two required)
⁵⁄₈in x ⁵⁄₈in x 2⁹⁄₃₂in
(16mm x 16mm x 58mm) long

HAT
1¹³⁄₃₂in x 1¹³⁄₃₂in x ²⁵⁄₃₂in
(36mm x 36mm x 20mm) thick

DRUMSTICK END
²³⁄₃₂in x ²³⁄₃₂in x 2¹⁵⁄₁₆in
(18mm x 18mm x 75mm) long
(Makes two)

NOSE
¹⁵⁄₃₂in x ¹⁵⁄₃₂in x 1²⁵⁄₃₂in
(12mm x 12mm x 45mm) long

WHEEL (four required)
2⁹⁄₃₂in x 2⁹⁄₃₂in x ²³⁄₃₂in
(58mm x 58mm x 18mm) thick

SHOE (two required)
¾in x ⅜in x 1⁹⁄₁₆in
(20mm x 10mm x 40mm) long

FRONT AXLE
¹³⁄₃₂in x ¹³⁄₃₂in x 4¹¹⁄₃₂in
(10mm x 10mm x 110mm) long

CENTRE SHAFT
¹⁵⁄₃₂in x ¹⁵⁄₃₂in x 5½in
(12mm x 12mm x 140mm) long

BACK AXLE
³¹⁄₃₂in x ³¹⁄₃₂in x 5½in
(25mm x 25mm x 140mm) long

RING HANDLE
2¾in x 2¾in x 1³¹⁄₃₂in
(70mm x 70mm x 50mm) long

In addition to these you will need the following items:

12in (300mm) x ³⁄₆₄in (1mm) long diameter strong wire or rod to make the connecting rods.

Two No.6 x 1in (25mm) long round head woodscrews. 2¹⁵⁄₁₆in (75mm) x ³⁄₃₂in (2½mm) diameter brass or steel rod.

Four No.4 x ½in (12mm) long round head woodscrews. Two ⁵⁄₁₆in (8mm) dowels x 3¹⁄₃₂in (25mm) long.

Four ¼in (6mm) dowels x 1⁹⁄₃₂in (15mm) long and one ¼in (6mm) dowel x ²³⁄₃₂in (18mm) long.

Four small felt or leather washers for the No.4 screws.

Three small screw eyes.

5in (125mm) long x ½in (12mm) wide x ⁵⁄₆₄in (2mm) thick mild steel strip and about 40in (1m) length of string.

ANATOMY OF A MUSIC MAN

MUSIC MAN

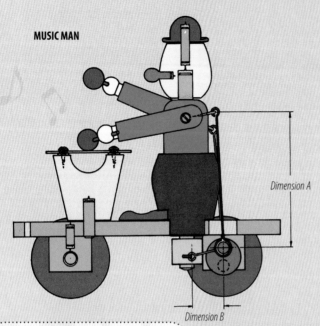

Dimension A

Dimension B

CONNECTING ROD

Dimension A and Dimension B

CONNECTING ROD

Dimensions A and B are measured after assembly. For further information on these dimensions refer to step 8 on page 153.

A ⁵⁄₆₄in (2mm) inside diameter

B ³⁄₆₄in (1mm) diameter

C ¹¹⁄₃₂in (9mm) diameter

PLATFORM

A 2 holes ⁵⁄₁₆in (8mm) diameter

B 2 slots ³⁄₁₆in (5mm) wide x ¾in (20mm) long

C ³⁄₈in (10mm)

D ⅞in (22mm)

E 1¾in (44mm)

F 4 holes ¼in (6mm) diameter x ⁵⁄₁₆in (8mm) deep

G ¾in (20mm)

H 1in (25mm) diameter

I 1in (25mm)

J 3¾in (95mm)

K ³⁄₁₆in (5mm)

L ¹³⁄₃₂in (10mm)

M 3⅜in (86mm)

N 1¹¹⁄₁₆in (43mm)

O ⁵⁄₃₂in (4mm) diameter

P ³⁄₈in (10mm)

Q 1⁹⁄₁₆in (40mm)

R 4¹¹⁄₃₂in (110mmm)

S 7½in (190mm)

PLATFORM
Viewed from underneath

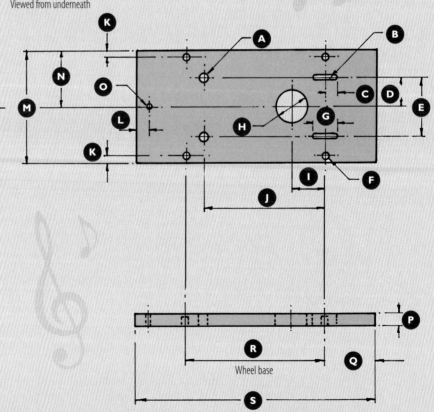

Wheel base

XYLOPHONE BASE

See xylophone drilling blank on page 142

XYLOPHONE BASE

- **A** 1⅞in (48mm)
- **B** 1⅜in (36mm)
- **C** ¹¹⁄₁₆in (18mm)
- **D** ¹⁹⁄₃₂in (15mm)
- **E** 1³⁄₁₆in (30mm)
- **F** 12.5°
- **G** 2¾in (70mm)
- **H** 1in (26mm)
- **I** ⅞in (22mm)
- **J** 2 holes ⁵⁄₆₄in (2mm) diameter x ¹³⁄₃₂in (10mm) deep
- **K** 1²⁵⁄₃₂in (45mm)
- **L** ¹⁵⁄₃₂in (12mm)
- **M** 1¾in (44mm)
- **N** 2 holes ⁵⁄₁₆in (8mm) diameter x ¹⁹⁄₃₂in (15mm) deep

XYLOPHONE PLATE

- **A** 2 holes drill ⁵⁄₃₂in (4mm) diameter
- **B** 1⅜in (36mm)
- **C** ½in (12mm)
- **D** ½in (12mm)
- **E** ⁵⁄₆₄in (2mm)
- **F** 2⅜in (60mm)
- **G** ¼in (6mm)

XYLOPHONE PLATE
(Two required)

BACK AXLE

- **A** 2⁵⁄₁₆in (64mm)
- **B** ¹⁹⁄₃₂in (15mm)
- **C** ⅛in (3mm)
- **D** ⁷⁄₁₆in (11mm) diameter
- **E** ½in (12mm) centres
- **F** ⅞in (22mm) diameter
- **G** ¾in (20mm)
- **H** 1¹³⁄₁₆in (46mm)
- **I** 4⅜in (110mm)
- **J** ⁵⁄₁₆in (8mm) diameter

AXLE BLOCK

- **A** 1³⁄₁₆in (30mm)
- **B** ¹⁹⁄₃₂in (15mm)
- **C** ⅜in (10mm) diameter
- **D** ¹⁹⁄₃₂in (15mm)
- **E** ²⁹⁄₃₂in (23mm)
- **F** ⅜in (10mm)
- **G** ¼in (6mm) diameter x ⁵⁄₁₆in (8mm) deep

BACK AXLE

Form a slight chamfer at each end

Centre line/datum

AXLE BLOCK

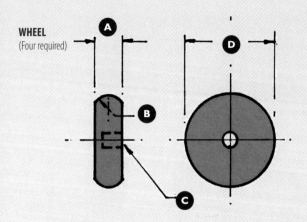

WHEEL
(Four required)

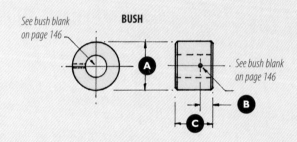

See bush blank on page 146

BUSH

See bush blank on page 146

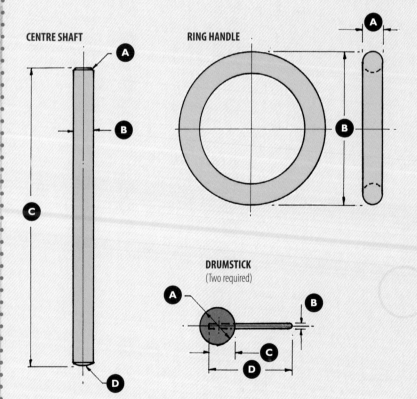

CENTRE SHAFT

RING HANDLE

DRUMSTICK
(Two required)

WHEEL

A ⅝in (16mm)

B ¹⁹⁄₃₂in (15mm) radius

C ⁵⁄₁₆in (8mm) diameter x ¹⁵⁄₃₂in (12mm) deep

D 2¹⁹⁄₃₂in (55mm) diameter

CENTRE SHAFT

A ³⁄₆₄in (1mm) x 45° chamfer

B ⅜in (10mm) diameter

C 5⁵⁄₁₆in (135mm)

D Domed end

BUSH

A ²⁵⁄₃₂in (20mm)

B ¼in (6mm)

C ²³⁄₃₂in (18mm)

RING HANDLE

A ⅜in (10mm) diameter

B 2⁹⁄₁₆in (65mm) diameter

DRUMSTICK

A ¹⁹⁄₃₂in (15mm) diameter

B ³⁄₃₂in (2.5mm) diameter

C ¹³⁄₃₂in (10mm)

D 1⅜in (35mm)

HEAD

A 1½in (38mm)
B 1in (25mm) diameter
C Blend radius
D ⁵⁄₃₂in (4mm) diameter x ⁵⁄₁₆in (8mm) deep
E ¾in (19mm) radius
F ²³⁄₃₂in (18mm)
G ⅝in (16mm)
H 1½in (38mm)

HANDS AND ARMS

A ¹³⁄₃₂in (10mm)
B ⁹⁄₁₆in (14mm)
C ¼in (6mm)
D 45°
E ⅛in (3mm)
F ¹³⁄₃₂in (10mm)
G ⁹⁄₁₆in (14mm) diameter
H 1²³⁄₃₂in (44mm)
I ⁵⁄₁₆in (8mm) radius

HAT

A 1¼in (33mm)
B ⅞in (22mm)
C ⁷⁄₁₆in (11mm) radius
D ⁵⁄₆₄in (2mm)
E ¼in (6mm) diameter x ¹³⁄₃₂in (10mm) deep
F ⅛in (3mm)
G ²³⁄₃₂in (18mm)

BODY

A 1³⁄₁₆in (30mm)
B ½in (12mm)
C ¹³⁄₃₂in (10mm) radius
D 3⁷⁄₃₂in (82mm)
E 1¹¹⁄₃₂in (34mm)
F 1⅞in (48mm)
G 1¹³⁄₁₆in (46mm)
H ³⁄₆₄in (1mm) x 45° chamfer
I 1in (25mm)
J ⁷⁄₁₆in (11mm)
K 1³⁄₃₂in (28mm)
L 2¹¹⁄₁₆in (68mm)
M 1¹³⁄₃₂in (36mm)

NOSE

A ³⁄₁₆in (5mm) radius
B ⁵⁄₃₂in (4mm) diameter
C ¼in (6mm)
D ¹⁵⁄₃₂in (12mm)

SHOE

A 1⅜in (35mm)
B ¹⁹⁄₃₂in (15mm)
C ²³⁄₃₂in (18mm)
D ¹¹⁄₃₂in (9mm) radius
E 1¼in (32mm)

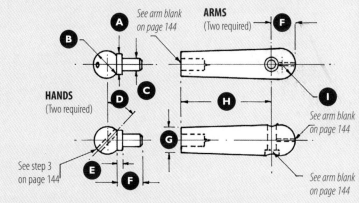

HANDS
(Two required)

See step 3 on page 144

See arm blank on page 144

ARMS
(Two required)

See arm blank on page 144

See arm blank on page 144

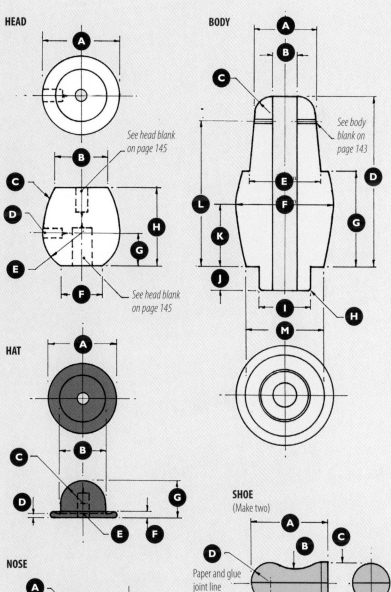

HEAD

See head blank on page 145

See head blank on page 145

BODY

See body blank on page 143

HAT

SHOE
(Make two)

Paper and glue joint line

NOSE

PLATFORM

1 Mark out and drill the holes and slots as detailed in the drawing on page 138.

AXLE BLOCK (4 required)

1 Cut out and drill the four axle blocks as shown in the detail drawing on page 139.

XYLOPHONE BASE

1 Mark out and drill the blank as shown below.

2 Set up the band saw to cut through the centre of the hole.

3 Angle the table to 12½° and cut the sloping sides. Refer to the detail drawing on page 139. Drill four pilot holes in the top edges, either side of the dished centre to take the plate securing screws.

BASE

XYLOPHONE BLANK DRILLING DETAIL

A Drill a 1in (25mm) diameter hole through blank

B 2in (50mm)

C 1in (25mm)

D 2¹¹⁄₃₂in (60mm)

E 1²⁵⁄₃₂in (45mm)

F 2¾in (70mm)

BODY

1 Mark out the positions and drill the two pilot holes as shown in the drawing below. Mark the diagonals at each end.

2 Mount the blank between centres on the lathe with the armholes at the headstock end. Rough down to a 1³¹⁄₃₂in (50mm) diameter cylinder and turn a dovetail spigot at the headstock end to suit your own compression chuck **1**.

3 Re-mount the blank in the compression chuck and fit a ½in (12mm) diameter drill in a chuck in the tailstock. Drill through the centre of the blank.

4 Bring the tailstock live centre into the hole you have just drilled and cut a 1in (25mm) diameter spigot x ⁷⁄₁₆in (11mm) long at the tailstock end. Turn a ³⁄₆₄in (1mm) x 45° chamfer on the end. Try the platform to check the fit **2**.

5 Reverse mount the blank in a small compression chuck using the 1in (25mm) spigot and bring up the tailstock into the centre hole. You can then complete the body profile, see the drawing on page 141 **3**. Sand and seal as necessary.

BODY

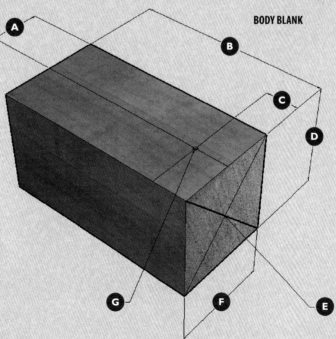

BODY BLANK

BODY BLANK

A 1¹⁄₃₂in (26mm)

B 3¾in (95mm)

C ⅝in (16mm)

D 2¹⁄₁₆in (52mm)

E Mark centres at each end

F 2¹⁄₁₆in (52mm)

G ⁵⁄₆₄in (2mm) diameter hole x ¹⁹⁄₃₂in (15mm) deep for arm pivot screw. Repeat in the opposite side for other arm

ARM BLANK

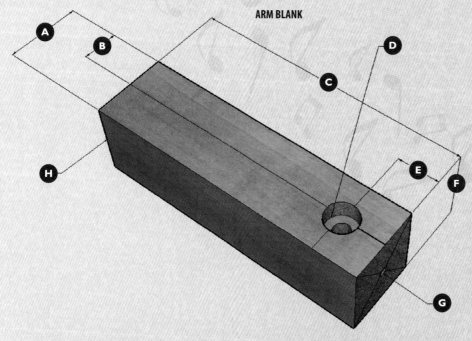

ARM BLANK

A ⅝in (16mm)

B ⁵⁄₁₆in (8mm)

C 2⁹⁄₃₂in (58mm)

D Drill ⁹⁄₃₂in (7mm) diameter x ⁵⁄₃₂in (4mm) deep, then ⁵⁄₃₂in (4mm) diameter through

E ¹⁵⁄₃₂in (12mm)

F ⅝in (16mm)

G Drill a ¹⁄₁₆in (1.5mm) diameter hole x ⁵⁄₁₆in (8mm) deep in the centre at this end

H Drill a ¼in (6mm) diameter hole x ¹⁵⁄₃₂in (12mm) deep in the centre at this end

HAND

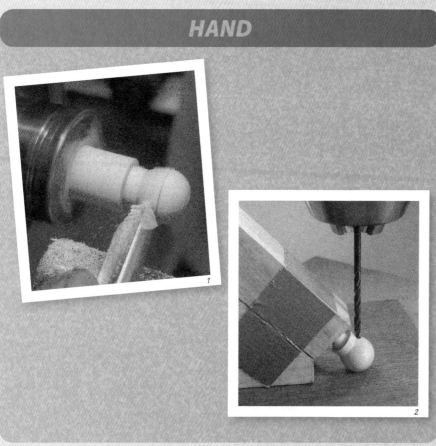

HAND (two required)

1 Prepare the arm blanks as shown in the drawing above. Use these blanks to hold the hand profiles so the holes can be drilled in the hands for the drumsticks.

2 Mount the hand blank directly in the jaws of a small compression chuck with sufficient material exposed to form the profile of one hand (see the detail drawing on page 141). Sand and seal. Make another hand from the same blank **1**.

3 Make a 45° angled block as shown **2** and dry fit the hand into the arm blank. Hold the assembly to drill the holes for the drumsticks. The drumstick should be a tight fit to help later adjustment before the final gluing. The tape shown in photograph **2** is simply for clarity.

HEAD

1 Mark the centres on the end grain. Drill a ⅜in (10mm) diameter x ²³⁄₃₂in (18mm) deep hole in one end and a ¼in (6mm) diameter hole x ¹³⁄₃₂in (10mm) deep in the other end as detailed in the drawing below.

2 Mount the blank on a ⅜in (10mm) diameter spigot chuck. Bring up the tailstock into the ¼in (6mm) hole.

3 Rough down to a cylinder and square up the ends to leave a length of 1½in (38mm). Mark a line ⅝in (16mm) from the headstock end to act as a guide for the maximum diameter. Then form the profile as detailed in the drawing on page 141. Sand and seal **1**. Leave the spigot chuck in place and remove the head.

4 Select a suitable point on the maximum diameter to drill a ⁵⁄₃₂in (4mm) diameter hole ready for the nose **2**.

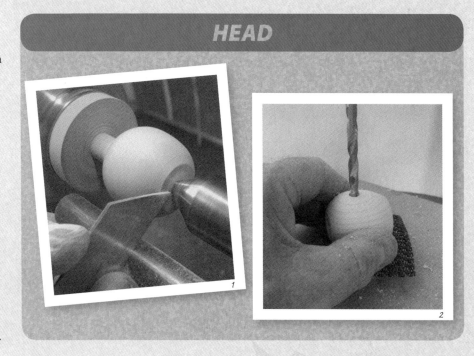

HEAD

HEAD BLANK

A 1⁹⁄₁₆in (40mm)

B 1⁹⁄₁₆in (40mm)

C 1⁹⁄₁₆in (40mm)

D Drill ⅜in (10mm) diameter x ²³⁄₃₂in (18mm) deep in the centre at this end. Drill into end grain. Drill ¼in (6mm) diameter x ¹³⁄₃₂in (10mm) deep in the centre at other end

HEAD BLANK

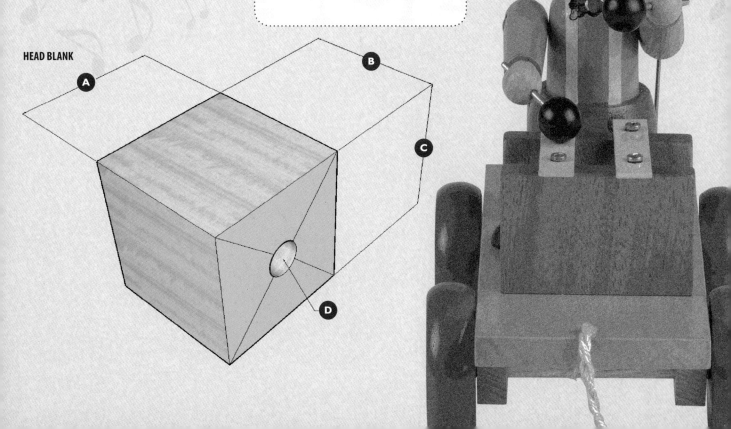

BUSH BLANK

BUSH

1 Mark out and drill the bush as shown in the drawing.

2 Mount the blank on the ⅜in (10mm) spigot chuck and turn down to a diameter of $^{25}/_{32}$in (20mm). Square up the ends to leave a length of $^{23}/_{32}$in (18mm), see the detail drawing on page 140. Sand and seal. Leave the spigot chuck in place.

BUSH BLANK

A ⅞in (22mm)

B $^7/_{16}$in (11mm)

C Drill a ¹⁄₁₆in (1.5mm) diameter hole x ¼in (6mm) deep

D $^{25}/_{32}$in (20mm)

E $^9/_{32}$in (7mm)

F ⅞in (22mm)

G Drill a ⅜in (10mm) diameter hole through blank

ARMS

ARMS (two required)

1 Turn the spigot chuck down to ¼in (6mm) diameter and mount the arm blank. Bring the tailstock up into the small hole drilled in the end.

2 Rough the blank down to a cylinder and form the profile, see the drawing on page 141. Sand and seal as required. Make the other arm in exactly the same way **1** . Leave the spigot chuck in place for the hat.

HAT

HAT

1 Mark the diagonals on one face of the blank and drill a ¼in (6mm) diameter hole x ¹³⁄₃₂in (10mm) deep. Remove the corners of the blank using the band saw to help with the turning.

2 Mount the blank on the spigot and rough down to a 1¹¹⁄₃₂in (34mm) diameter 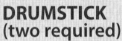.

3 Square up the ends and, leaving ⅛in (3mm) for the brim, reduce the remainder of the blank to a diameter of ⅞in (22mm).

4 Radius the end to finish the profile, see the drawing on page 141. Sand and seal . The spigot chuck can now be removed. Keep all the parts safely in a box awaiting assembly.

DRUMSTICK (two required)

1 Mount the blank directly in the jaws of a small compression chuck with sufficient material exposed for the ¹⁹⁄₃₂in (15mm) diameter sphere, plus ³⁄₁₆in (5mm) or so for cutting off.

2 Mount a Jacobs-type chuck in the tailstock and drill a hole in the end of the blank to suit the diameter of the drumstick rod x ¹³⁄₃₂in (10mm) deep. See the drawing on page 140.

3 Bring the tailstock live centre into the hole and turn a ¹⁹⁄₃₂in (15mm) diameter sphere. There is enough material to make the second profile in exactly the same way .

4 Cut the drumstick rod into two equal 1⅜in (35mm) lengths and glue these into the ends. When the glue has set, mount the rod in a Jacobs-type chuck in the headstock. Sand and seal the spheres. Remove the completed drumsticks and ensure that the end of the rod is nicely rounded to remove all sharp edges. Place the parts in your box.

NOSE

1 Make the nose in a similar fashion to that used to make the hands, see drawing on page 141.

DRUMSTICK

WHEEL (four required)

1 Mark the diagonals on one face of the blank and scribe a 2³⁄₁₆in (56mm) diameter around the centre point using a pencil.

2 Drill a ⁵⁄₁₆in (8mm) x ¹⁵⁄₃₂in (12mm) deep hole in the centre and cut out the circle on the band saw using the pencil line as a guide.

3 Mount the blank on a ⁵⁄₁₆in (8mm) diameter dowel in the jaws of a Jacobs-type chuck or a spigot chuck and place a cover on the tailstock live centre **1** .

4 Use a gouge to form the outside profile of the wheel, see the drawing on page 140. Square up the inside face with a parting tool **2** .

5 Clean up the outside face of the wheel to leave a thickness of ⁵⁄₈in (16mm) **3** .

6 Make another three wheels. Use a simple template to keep all the profiles the same **4** . Sand and seal as necessary.

WHEEL

SHOES

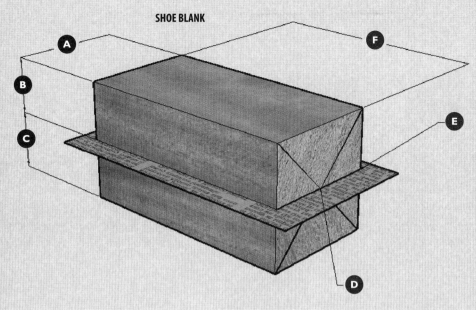

SHOE BLANK

SHOE BLANK

A ¾in (20mm)

B ⅜in (10mm)

C ⅜in (10mm)

D Mark exact centre to ensure both shoes will be identical

E Paper and glue joint

F 1⁹⁄₁₆in (40mm)

SHOES

1 Cut the blanks to size and make the composite shoe blank as shown in the drawing above. Leave this to cure fully overnight.

2 Mount the blank between centres . Note the ring centre on the point of the tailstock to reduce the pressure on the joint line.

3 Stand to one side and switch on the lathe. Allow it to run for about a minute then switch it off to check that the joint has not opened up. Use full face protection and turn the profile, see the drawing on page 141. Sand, seal and remove from the lathe.

4 Use a sharp blade to open the joint and clean off the paper. Sand the rear face of each shoe to fit the body profile 2.

FRONT AXLE

1 Mount the blank between centres and turn down to a ⁵⁄₁₆in (8mm) x 4¹¹⁄₃₂in (110mm) long dowel with a slight chamfer at each end.

CENTRE SHAFT

1 As above, mount the blank between centres and turn down to a ⅜in (10mm) x 5⁵⁄₁₆in (135mm) dowel. See the drawing on page 140. Cut a slight chamfer on one end and a domed profile on the other.

BACK AXLE

BACK AXLE

This is the offset turning mentioned earlier. It should not present you with any problems, even if you have never turned off-centre before. However, losing concentration or forgetting that the piece is spinning in an eccentric manner can result in serious injury. A good rule to apply to all your turning is never place your fingers between the work piece and the tool rest.

1 Mark the blank in accordance with the drawing on page 151. I am using a piece of European beech (*Fagus sylvatica*) for its qualities of strength and close straight grain. Indent the three centres at each end with a bradawl. Ensure that the centres are on corresponding diagonals.

2 Mount the blank between centres on the centre point each end (centre b in the drawing). Use a roughing gouge to turn the square blank down to a cylinder, and smooth with a skew chisel to a diameter of ⅞in (22mm). Sand and seal.

3 Mark a centre line around the blank in pencil and mark the divisions for the various sections using the centre line as your datum, see the drawing on page 139. I have coloured the offset cranks red and green for clarity 1 .

4 Re-mount the blank on the same offset centre each end. Make sure the tailstock is fully supporting the blank and move the tool rest to clear the new swing of the blank. Test this by spinning the blank by hand before switching it on. Set the speed to about 1,100rpm and use a parting tool to cut one of the cranks. Watch the top edge of the turning. When the ghosting stops and the profile becomes clear, the diameter should be ⁷⁄₁₆in (11mm).

5 Mark the centre of this crank for the ⅛in (3mm) wide shoulder and continue to turn the remainder of the crank down to ⁵⁄₁₆in (8mm) diameter each side of the shoulder 2 . Remove the tool rest, sand and seal the crank. Keep your fingers well away from the eccentric parts of the turning.

6 Cut a small block of timber the exact width of the crank and tape it firmly into place as shown 3 . This will prevent the blank flexing when the offset load, which is required to turn the other crank, is applied.

7 Re-mount the blank in the opposite centres and repeat the procedure to turn the other crank. There is no need to turn the shoulder on this side. Cut another block to fit the width of this crank and tape into position.

8 Re-mount the blank back in the centre mark and ensure the blocks clear the tool rest. Turn the two ends down to ⁵⁄₁₆in (8mm) diameter 4 .

9 Part in slightly each end equally around the centre point to give a length of 4⅜in (110mm) with a slight chamfer at each end. Sand and seal, keeping the ends clear of sealer where the wheels are to be glued on. Remove from the lathe and cut off the waste as necessary. Remove the blocks.

RING HANDLE

1 Mount the blank between centres and rough down to a diameter of 2¹⁹⁄₃₂in (66mm). Then cut a dovetail spigot to suit your own compression chuck.

2 Re-mount the blank, see the drawing on page 140. Using a parting tool create a ³⁄₈in (10mm) wide x ³⁄₈in (10mm) deep flange **1a**. Remember to leave enough space to get a ring cutter or a spindle gouge in to form the ring **1b**.

3 Sand and seal before parting off the ring. A little sanding will be necessary on the inside face after parting off.

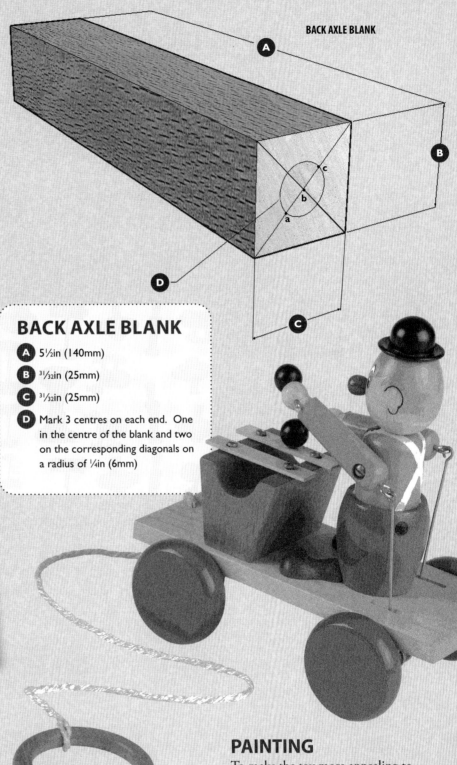

BACK AXLE BLANK

RING HANDLE

1a

1b

BACK AXLE BLANK

A 5½in (140mm)

B 3¹⁄₃₂in (25mm)

C 3¹⁄₃₂in (25mm)

D Mark 3 centres on each end. One in the centre of the blank and two on the corresponding diagonals on a radius of ¼in (6mm)

XYLOPHONE PLATES

1 Cut the metal strip into two equal 2³⁄₈in (60mm) long strips and drill the holes as shown in the drawing on page 139.

PAINTING

To make the toy more appealing to young children, I am going to paint the body, arms, the wheels and the two xylophone plates. I shall also paint on the eyes, mouth and hair before assembly. All this is something you can decide yourself, but whatever type of finish you decide on, it is important to keep the surfaces of parts which will be glued together free of any finish.

CONNECTING RODS

With all the parts made and painted where necessary, you can start to build the toy. There are still a couple of important measurements to determine the length of the connecting rods, so follow the procedure here and refer to the anatomy drawing.

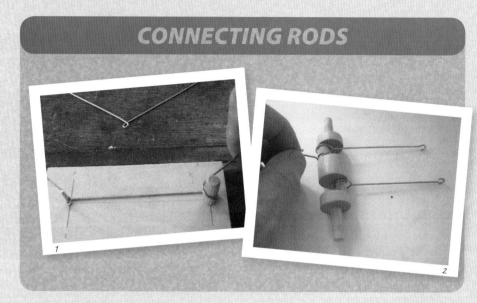

CONNECTING RODS

1 Glue the two front axle blocks with their dowels into position on the underside of the platform. Glue one of the wheels onto the front axle and fit this to the front blocks. Glue on the other front wheel and ensure the wheels rotate freely.

2 Glue the two ⁵⁄₁₆in (8mm) dowels into the xylophone base and glue the base to the platform. Fit the xylophone plates to the base using No.4 screws and felt or leather washers. The plates must be loose enough to ring, so do not tighten the screws fully, but ensure the assembly is secure.

3 Fit a screw eye into the shoulder end of each arm and fit the arms to the body using No.6 screws. Ensure that the points of the screws do not interfere with the centre hole in the body. Use a round file if necessary to take off the points. The arms should rise and fall freely without any side play. Glue the body onto the platform facing forwards.

4 Glue the bush onto the domed end of the centre shaft, leaving about ⅛in (3mm) protruding. Fit the screw eye into the small hole in the bush and glue the nose into the head. The next items are not glued yet, as they will need to be taken apart again after the measurements for *Dimension A* and *Dimension B* are determined, see anatomy drawing.

5 Fit the drumsticks into the hands and the hands into the arms. These items need to be tight enough to remain in position when adjusted. Rest the drumsticks on the plates in a natural looking position.

6 Fit the two remaining axle blocks, with their dowels onto the ends of the back axle and push on the two wheels. Fit the blocks into their respective dowel holes on the platform and make sure the blocks are sitting flush with the platform.

7 Fit the centre shaft and bush assembly up through the hole in the body and fit the head onto the top of the shaft. Leave ⅛in (2mm) vertical play to ensure the head turns freely. The head should face forwards with the screw eye at 90° as drawn.

8 With everything in position, turn the back axle so the cranks are arranged vertically. Measure the centres to determine *Dimension A*. In my case, the measurement is 3½in (87mm). Now measure *Dimension B*. My measurement here is 1in (25mm). Carefully disassemble all the dry fitted parts.

9 A simple jig can now be made to bend the wire into the connecting rods, see the drawing on page 138. The jig is a board with a ¹⁄₁₆in (2mm) diameter pin and a ⁵⁄₁₆in (8mm) dowel set in at the required centres. Wrap the wire around the pin at one end and the dowel to form the connecting rods 1 . You will need two at *Dimension A* and one at *Dimension B*. Form the coils open like a corkscrew, so they can be slipped over the axle cranks and screw eyes. Cut off any excess wire and ensure the inside diameter of the coil is not too tight on the axle.

10 Fit the rods to the axle 2 and fit the short rod to the screw eye in the centre shaft/bush assembly. Use a small pair of pliers to close the coils on the rods after assembly. Glue the dowels to the axle blocks and then fit the blocks onto the axle as before. Feed the two long connecting rods through the slots in the platform and the centre shaft into the hole in the body. Apply adhesive to the dowels and the top of the axle blocks, then

fix into position. Glue the head onto the top of the shaft, making sure that the face is forward with the screw eye at 90°. Fit the small ends of the connecting rods onto the screw eyes in each arm and close the loops. Glue on the back wheels and ensure everything is free to turn.

11 Adjust the angle of the hands and the position of the drumsticks so they just touch the plates when the respective crank is at its highest. When you are satisfied with the action, glue in both the hands and the drumsticks.

12 Glue on the hat and give the whole toy, including the ring handle, a spray coat of melamine. Finally, tie the string to the platform and the handle.

This toy brings back many memories for me because I was given one as a child. It was made to look like a man in a coat and hat, which were painted on.

I also recall seeing a cross-country vehicle from the 1930s which had legs and felloes instead of wheels, and walked across rough or soft ground. I suspect that the toy was a development of this rather wacky machine. Whatever the origin, it is a simple but clever device to make and will amuse both adults and children alike.

There are certain advantages to making the toy in the form of a penguin. One is that the action is more of a waddle and suggestive of penguins and, by using appropriate timbers, there is no need to paint the toy to make clear its identity.

WALKING PENGUIN

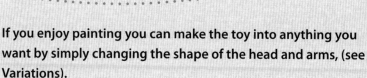

If you enjoy painting you can make the toy into anything you want by simply changing the shape of the head and arms, (see Variations).

The toy's ability to walk successfully is partly due to keeping the centre of gravity as low as possible. This is achieved by hollowing out the head and using quite large feet.

Many of the parts are drilled prior to turning as this is easier and more accurate. If the blanks are cut and prepared square, it will help to keep the legs and body at 90° to the pivot.

A simple jig will be needed to assemble the legs and feet, then to sand the necessary profile to form the felloes, see the drawing on page 165. After sanding, all the parts are sealed with an acrylic sanding sealer and finished with several coats of acrylic lacquer before final assembly.

Cutting List

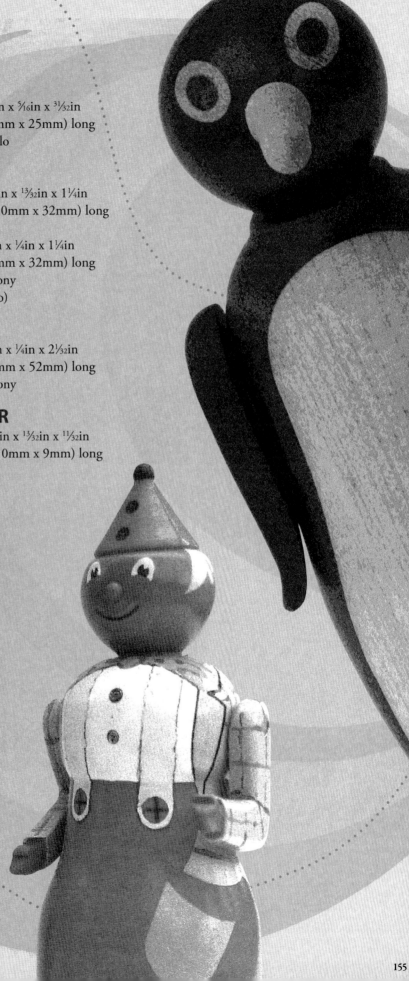

COMPOSITE BODY

1 piece 2in x 1⅝in x 4in
(50mm x 40mm x 100mm) long
African ebony (*Diospyros crassiflora*)
1 piece 2in x ⅜in x 4in
(50mm x 10mm x 100mm) long
sycamore (*Acer pseudoplatanus*)
Glue these two pieces together
to make one blank 2in x 2in x 4in
(50mm x 50mm x 100mm) long

HEAD

1 piece 1¼in x 1¼in x 1½in
(32mm x 32mm x 38mm) long
African ebony

LEGS

2 pieces ½in x ½in x 4⅛in
(12mm x 12mm x 105mm) long
beech (*Fagus sylvatica*)

ARMS

2 pieces ⅝in x ¹³⁄₃₂in x 1²⁵⁄₃₂in
(16mm x 10mm x 45mm) long
African ebony

FELLOES

2 pieces ²⁵⁄₃₂in x ²³⁄₃₂in x 2²⁹⁄₃₂in
(20mm x 18mm x 74mm) long
Pau amarello (*Euxylophora paraensis*).

Note: this wood is also known as
Brazilian satinwood or sateenwood.
It is a bright clear yellow with a lustrous
deep ribbon figure and is useful as a
basic colour for turned items. It should
not be confused with other timbers
called amarello (*Aspidosperma peroba*,
Plathymenia reticulata and *Machaerium
villosum*).

BEAK

1 piece ⁵⁄₁₆in x ⁵⁄₁₆in x ³¹⁄₃₂in
(8mm x 8mm x 25mm) long
Pau amarello

EYES

1 piece ¹³⁄₃₂in x ¹³⁄₃₂in x 1¼in
(10mm x 10mm x 32mm) long
sycamore
1 piece ¼in x ¼in x 1¼in
(6mm x 6mm x 32mm) long
African ebony
(Makes two)

PIVOT

1 piece ¼in x ¼in x 2¹⁄₃₂in
(6mm x 6mm x 52mm) long
African ebony

SPACER

1 piece ¹³⁄₃₂in x ¹³⁄₃₂in x ¹¹⁄₃₂in
(10mm x 10mm x 9mm) long
beech

**Marking out the dark wood blanks
is easier if masking tape is first
applied to the blank, making the
lines easily visible.**

ANATOMY OF A PENGUIN

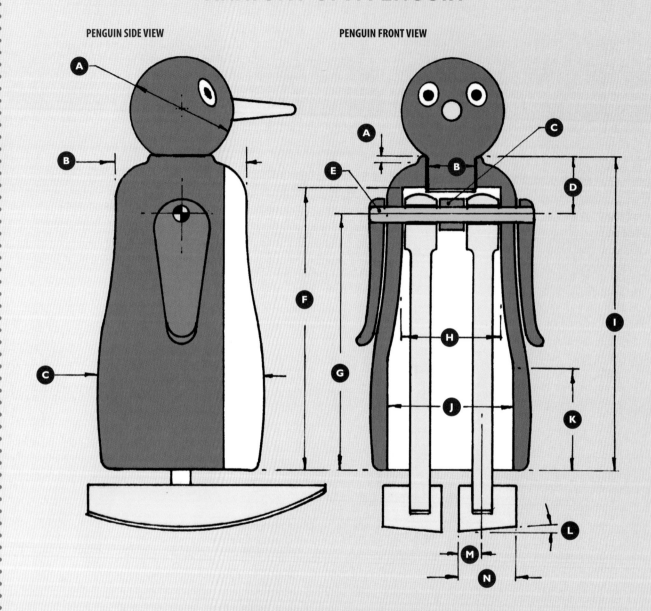

PENGUIN SIDE VIEW

PENGUIN FRONT VIEW

PENGUIN SIDE VIEW

Ⓐ 1³⁄₁₆in (30mm) diameter

Ⓑ 1⁹⁄₁₆in (40mm) diameter

Ⓒ 1⅞in (48mm) diameter

PENGUIN FRONT VIEW

Ⓐ ⁵⁄₆₄in (2mm) x ²⁵⁄₃₂in (20mm) diameter collar

Ⓑ ⁹⁄₁₆in (14mm) diameter

Ⓒ ¹¹⁄₃₂in (9mm) long spacer

Ⓓ ¹⁹⁄₃₂in (15mm)

Ⓔ ⁵⁄₃₂in (4mm) diameter x 2¹⁄₃₂in (52mm) long pivot

Ⓕ 3⁵⁄₁₆in (84mm), drilling depth at 1³⁄₁₆in (30mm) diameter

Ⓖ 2¹⁵⁄₁₆in (75mm)

Ⓗ 1³⁄₁₆in (30mm) diameter

Ⓘ 3¹⁷⁄₃₂in (90mm)

Ⓙ 1½in (38mm) diameter

Ⓚ 1³⁄₁₆in (30mm), drilling depth at 1½in (38mm) diameter

Ⓛ 2°

Ⓜ ⁹⁄₃₂in (7mm)

Ⓝ ²⁵⁄₃₂in (20mm)

LEG
(Two required)

See leg blank on page 163

Use assembly/sanding jig when gluing leg to felloe

Use assembly/sanding jig to form profile

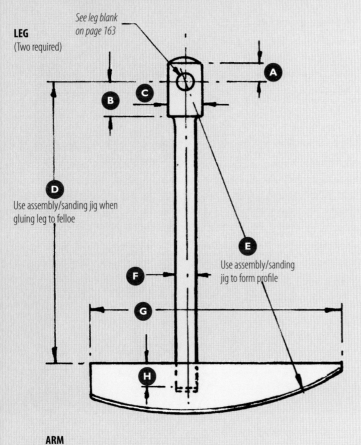

ARM
(Two required)

Sand this face to match body profile

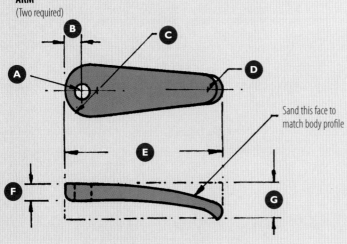

BEAK

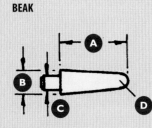

EYE

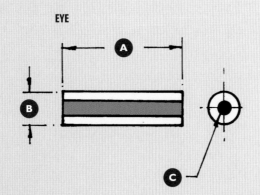

SPACER

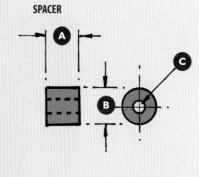

LEG

- **A** ³⁄₁₆in (5mm)
- **B** 1³⁄₃₂in (10mm)
- **C** 1³⁄₃₂in (10mm) diameter
- **D** 3⁵⁄₃₂in (80mm)
- **E** 3¾in (95mm) radius
- **F** ¼in (6mm) diameter
- **G** 2²⁹⁄₃₂in (74mm)
- **H** ⁵⁄₁₆in (8mm)

ARM

- **A** ⁵⁄₃₂in (4mm) diameter
- **B** ³⁄₁₆in (5mm)
- **C** ⁵⁄₁₆in (8mm) radius
- **D** ⁵⁄₃₂in (4mm) radius
- **E** 1¾in (45mm)
- **F** ³⁄₁₆in (5mm)
- **G** 1³⁄₃₂in (10mm)

BEAK

- **A** 2⁵⁄₃₂in (20mm)
- **B** ¼in (6mm) diameter
- **C** ⁵⁄₃₂in (4mm) diameter
- **D** ⁵⁄₆₄in (2mm) radius

EYE

- **A** 1¼in (32mm)
- **B** ⁹⁄₃₂in (7mm) diameter
- **C** ⁵⁄₃₂in (4mm) diameter

SPACER

- **A** ¹¹⁄₃₂in (9mm)
- **B** 1³⁄₃₂in (10mm) diameter
- **C** ⁵⁄₃₂in (4mm) diameter

BODY

1 Glue the two pieces of the body together to make one composite blank 2in (50mm) x 2in (50mm) x 4in (100mm) long. When the glue has cured, mark out the blank as shown in the drawing on page 159 and drill a ⁵⁄₃₂in (4mm) diameter hole through the blank (1). This hole must be drilled at 90° to the sides of the blank. Mark the diagonals at each end to locate the centres.

2 Mount the blank between centres. While wearing full face protection, rough down to a cylinder, just removing all flat surfaces (2). Square up the ends with a parting tool.

3 Re-mount the blank into the compression jaws of your chuck with the ⁵⁄₃₂in (4mm) diameter pivot hole at the headstock end. Bring up the tailstock centre into the centre mark, before fully tightening the jaws. Do not worry about marking the body with the jaws as this will be further reduced later.

4 Reduce the length of the blank to 2¹⁵⁄₁₆in (75mm) from the centre of the pivot hole. Use a sharp 1½in (38mm) diameter sawtooth bit to drill a 1³⁄₁₆in (30mm) deep hole (3).

5 Drill another hole 1³⁄₁₆in (30mm) diameter to a depth of 3³⁄₁₆in (84mm) from the bottom edge. Then drill through the remainder of the blank using a ⁹⁄₁₆in (14mm) diameter drill. Drill all the holes slowly with very sharp drill bits to avoid overheating the wood and destroying the glue joint.

6 Use a round nose scraper to blend together the two larger diameter holes, see anatomy drawing (4a). Mark pencil lines on the outside profile to indicate where the two diameters blend together (4b). Seal the inside and bottom face (4c).

TOP TIP

To clear shavings or dust from awkward places such as this, use a 20in (50cm) length of soft plastic tubing (sold by motor car accessory shops for bleeding brakes and so on). Place one end in the hole and blow. A couple of puffs should clean out the cavity without covering you in dust.

SAFETY NOTE

When turning composite blanks, stand to one side when first switching on the lathe. Allow the blank to spin for around a minute or so before switching it off. Make sure the joints have not opened up before continuing to turn.

BODY

1

2

3

4a

4b

4c

BODY BLANK

A 2in (50mm)

B 1⅝in (40mm)

C 3⁵⁄₃₂in (80mm)

D 4in (100mm)

E 1in (25mm)

BODY BLANK

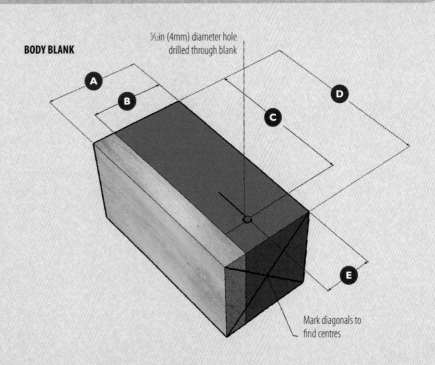

⁵⁄₃₂in (4mm) diameter hole drilled through blank

A

B

C

D

E

Mark diagonals to find centres

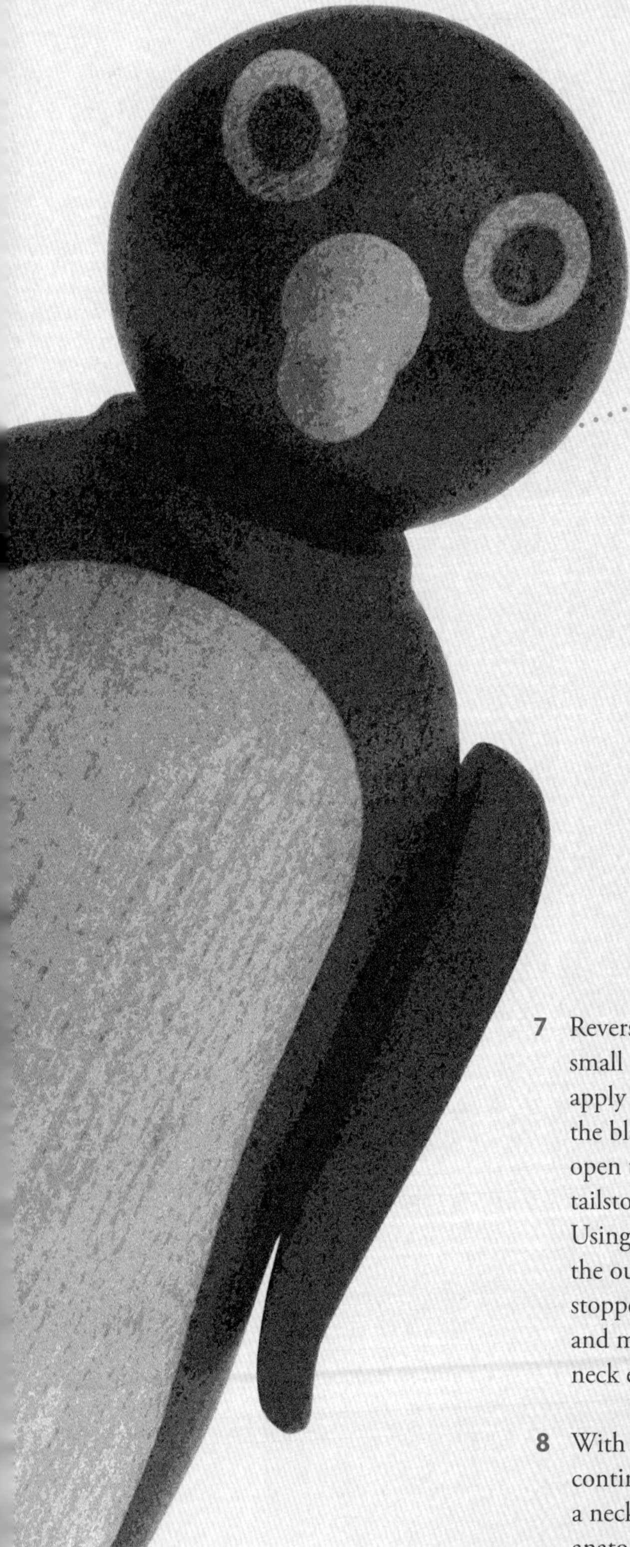

BODY

5

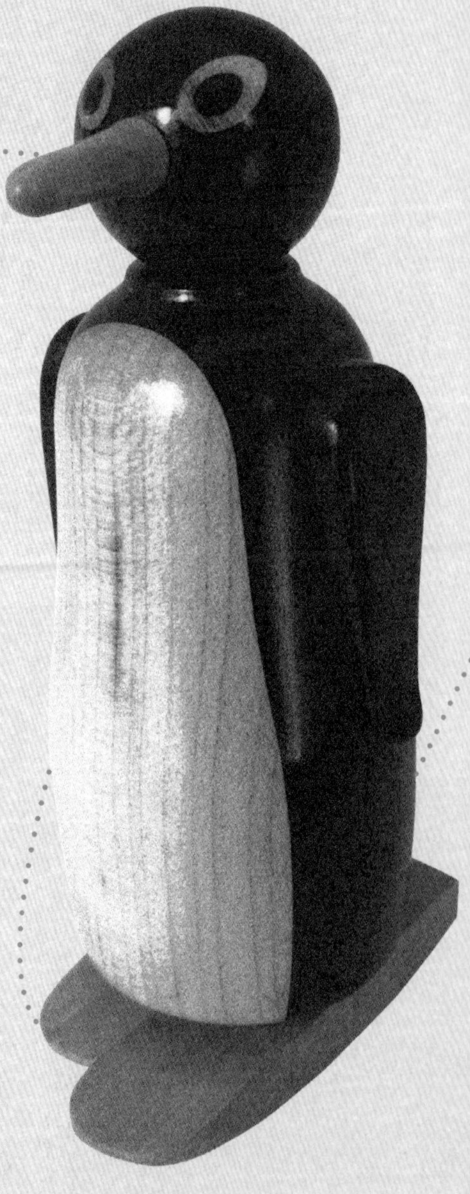

7 Reverse mount the blank onto a small expansion jaw chuck. Only apply sufficient pressure to drive the blank, as too much force will open the glue joint. Bring up the tailstock centre into the neck hole. Using a skew or spindle gouge, form the outside profile. With the lathe stopped, withdraw the tailstock and measure the thickness of the neck end **5** .

8 With the tailstock back in position, continue turning the profile to leave a neck thickness of ¼in (6mm), see anatomy drawing. Sand and seal as necessary. Both these timbers cut beautifully with sharp chisels. If you can avoid the need to sand, there will be no danger of the rather oily blackwood contaminating the colour of the sycamore. Remove the blank from the lathe and keep safely to one side, ideally in a box on your bench to await final assembly.

3 Mount the blackwood in the same chuck. You will need to round off the corners with a sharp blade if mounting in a three-jaw chuck. Turn the blank down to a dowel ⁵⁄₃₂in (4mm) in diameter which will fit inside the sycamore sleeve **3** .

4 Glue the dowel into the sleeve and saw through to make two ¹⁹⁄₃₂in (15mm) long eye blanks.

EYES

1 Drill a ⁵⁄₃₂in (4mm) diameter hole through the centre of the sycamore blank from end to end **1** .

2 Use a simple mandrel and mount the blank in a Jacobs-type chuck. I have used a ⁵⁄₃₂in (4mm) x 1⁹⁄₁₆in (40mm) long cross head bolt and nut. Bring up the tailstock into the cross head centre and turn the outside down to ⁹⁄₃₂in (7mm) diameter. Do not worry about the ends being square as these will be turned later. Remove from the lathe and take the mandrel out **2** .

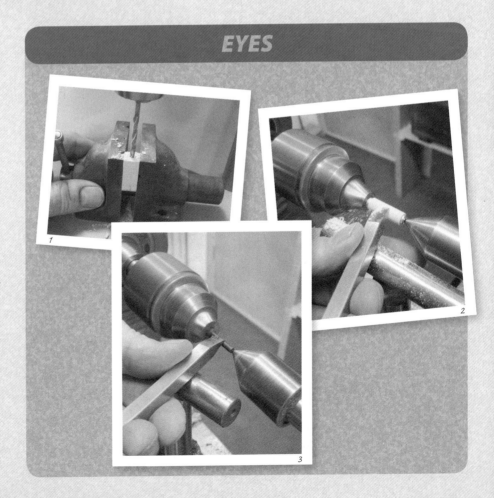

EYES

HEAD BLANK

A	1¼in (32mm)	**E**	1¼in (32mm)
B	¹¹⁄₃₂in (9mm)	**F**	⁵⁄₁₆in (8mm)
C	⅝in (16mm)	**G**	⁵⁄₁₆in (8mm)
D	1½in (38mm)	**H**	⅝in (16mm)

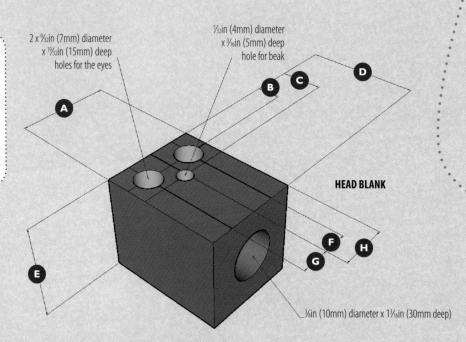

2 x ⁹⁄₃₂in (7mm) diameter x ¹⁹⁄₃₂in (15mm) deep holes for the eyes

⁵⁄₃₂in (4mm) diameter x ³⁄₁₆in (5mm) deep hole for beak

HEAD BLANK

⅜in (10mm) diameter x 1³⁄₁₆in (30mm deep)

HEAD

1 Mark out the head blank as shown in the drawing **1**.

2 Drill all the holes as detailed and glue in the two eyes **2**.

3 Mount the blank between centres with the tailstock in the ⅜in (10mm) diameter end hole **3**.

4 Round down the blank with a roughing gouge and form a ⁹⁄₁₆in (14mm) diameter x ⁵⁄₁₆in (8mm) long spigot at the tailstock end. Check that the neck fits in the body **4**.

5 Start from the centre line of the beak hole and form a radius down to the spigot **5**.

6 Reverse mount the blank with the spigot in a small compression jaw chuck and turn the remainder of the head profile. Seal the timber and put in the parts box **6**.

HEAD

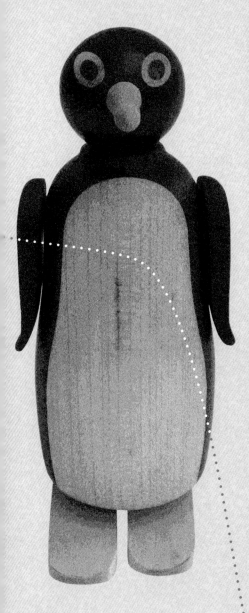

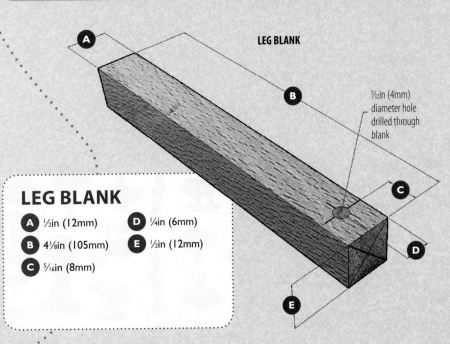

LEGS

1 Mark and drill the two leg blanks as detailed in the drawing **1** .

2 Mount the blanks between centres **2a** and turn the profile, see the drawing on page 157 **2b** .

3 Sand and seal as necessary.

4 Measure the cut off point (this will be 3¹⁵⁄₃₂in (88mm) from the hole centre) and reduce the ends to as small as safely possible **3** .

5 Remove from the lathe and cut off the waste using a sharp blade.

LEG BLANK

⁵⁄₃₂in (4mm) diameter hole drilled through blank

LEG BLANK

A ½in (12mm)   **D** ¼in (6mm)

B 4⅛in (105mm)   **E** ½in (12mm)

C ⁵⁄₁₆in (8mm)

FELLOES

1 Mark out and drill the blanks as detailed in the drawing below. Make sure you have made one left and one right foot (**1**).

2 There is no turning to do on these felloes. Mark out a radius on the front end of each blank as a sanding guide and sand a radiused end (**2**).

3 Sand the top and side faces to remove any pencil lines. Then seal the timber.

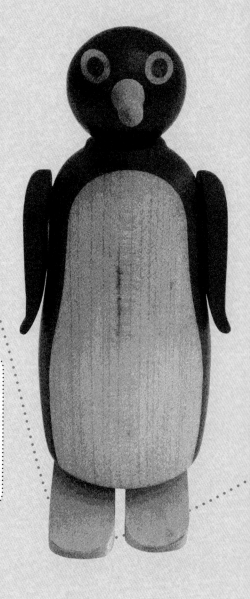

FELLOES

1

2

FELLOES BLANK

A $^{25}/_{32}$in (20mm)   **D** $1^{3}/_{32}$in (28mm)

B $^{9}/_{32}$in (7mm)   **E** $2^{29}/_{32}$in (74mm)

C $^{23}/_{32}$in (18mm)

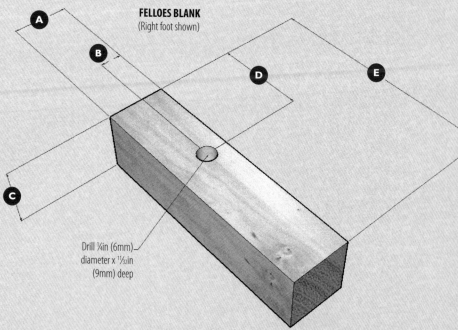

FELLOES BLANK
(Right foot shown)

Drill ¼in (6mm) diameter x $^{11}/_{32}$in (9mm) deep

LEGS

LEG AND FELLOES ASSEMBLY

The assembly is quite straightforward and will be more accurate if the small jig is made. This jig is a multi-purpose item and will also enable the setting up of the sanding angle and the sanding of the bottom profile on the felloes.

ASSEMBLY/ SANDING JIG

A 2½in (63.5mm)		**E** 90°	
B 1³⁄₁₆in (30mm)		**F** 2¹¹⁄₃₂in (60mm)	
C 3¹⁵⁄₁₆in (100mm)		**G** ⁵⁄₁₆in (8mm)	
D 3⁵⁄₃₂in (80mm)			

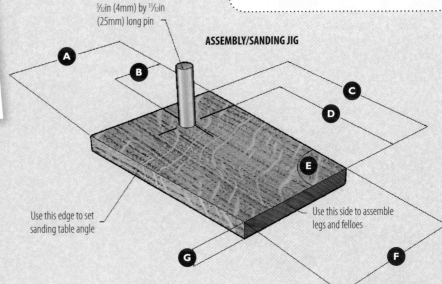

⁵⁄₃₂in (4mm) by 3¹⁄₃₂in (25mm) long pin

ASSEMBLY/SANDING JIG

Use this edge to set sanding table angle

Use this side to assemble legs and felloes

1. Make up the jig as detailed above. Ensure the pin is glued in at right angles to the platform.

2. Place the jig on a flat surface. Fit one of the legs onto the pin with the end of the leg over the edge of the platform that is 3⁵⁄₃₂in (80mm) from the centre of the pin. Apply some glue to the joint and fit the felloe onto the leg. This jig will ensure that the top of each felloe is 3⁵⁄₃₂in (80mm) from the centre of the pivot and the pivot rod and felloe are 90° to each other.

3. Repeat the procedure with the other leg so you finish with a matching pair of legs.

SANDING THE FELLOES

1   After assembling the two legs, you will need to sand the bottom surface of the felloes at a 3¾in (95mm) radius and also at a 2° angle.

2   Set up your sanding table to give a 2° angle. Use the jig to set the angle of your sanding table **1**.

3   Use the assembly/sanding jig placed flat on the table of your sander with the pin at a distance of about 4⅛in (105mm) from the face of the abrasive disc. Clamp securely into position **2**.

4   Place one leg assembly onto the pin. With the sander switched on, swing the leg assembly slowly across the face of the abrasive disc. Do not press down on the leg as this may flex and alter the angle of the felloe **3**.

5   Repeat with the other leg at the same setting.

6   Reset the distance of the pin to 3¾in (95mm) from the face of the disc and repeat as above. Remember you are making one right and one left foot. The entire bottom surface of the felloes should now be radiused and at an angle of 2° **4**.

7   Seal the bottom surfaces and place in the parts box.

SANDING THE FELLOES

SPACER

1 Drill a ⁵⁄₃₂in (4mm) diameter hole through the blank and mount on the same mandrel you used for the eye sleeve. Turn a ¹³⁄₃₂in (10mm) diameter x ¹¹⁄₃₂in (9mm) long spacer, see anatomy drawing. Seal and put safely in your parts box.

PIVOT

1 Turn a ⁵⁄₃₂in (4mm) dowel x 2¹⁄₃₂in (52mm) long to act as the pivot for the felloes. The turning will be exactly the same procedure you used for the centre of the eye. Seal and then put with the other parts.

ARMS

1 Drill a ⁵⁄₃₂in (4mm) diameter hole through the blank as shown in the drawing on page 157.

2 The arms are formed by sanding. Mark out the profile on the blanks ❶ . The inside of the arm will follow the profile of the body. Fit the pivot into the body and sand the profile until it fits nicely along the body when mounted on the pivot ❷ . Do not glue anything yet. Sand the other arm and seal with sanding sealer. Then place all the parts together ready for assembly.

BEAK

1 Mount the blank in a small chuck and form the profile, see the drawing on page 157.

2 Glue the beak into position in the head.

ARMS

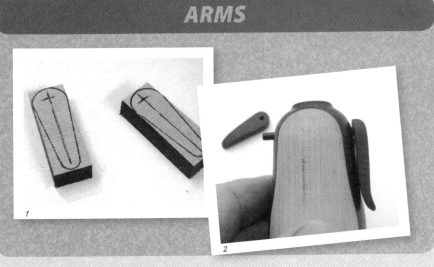

1

2

BEAK

ASSEMBLY

1 Start with the two legs, pivot and spacer. The legs need to swing freely on the pivot, but with very little side movement. The inside faces of the felloes must not touch each other when assembled **1** . Use a needle file or tightly rolled abrasive paper to enlarge the hole diameter in the leg just enough to allow the leg to swing forward and back. Make the same adjustment to the hole in the spacer so that assembly inside the body will be easier.

2 Keep checking the movement, removing only sufficient material to allow the legs to swing freely with a gap between the felloes. If you go too far and the inside of the felloes touch, the toy will not walk. You can remove some of the material from the inside face of the felloes to get it walking again.

3 The whole toy is now ready to be assembled. Do not glue any parts together until the tuning up has been completed and the toy is walking correctly.

4 Push the pivot rod through one of the holes in the side of the body. This should not require excessive force and may need a little relieving to push gently through. It is better to have everything a bit tight to start with and to remove material, rather than to have it too loose and have to remake parts.

5 With the end of the pivot rod visible through the hole in the neck, place the appropriate leg up into the body and thread it onto the pivot rod. Use a pair of tweezers or fine pointed pliers to thread on the spacer and push the pivot through the other leg hole and through to the other side of the body **2** . Hold up the body and check that the legs still swing freely, almost like ringing a bell. Adjust as necessary until the action is smooth.

6 Push in the head, making sure there is clearance between the end of the spigot and the top of the legs.

7 Push the arms onto each end of the pivot rod and you are ready to test run.

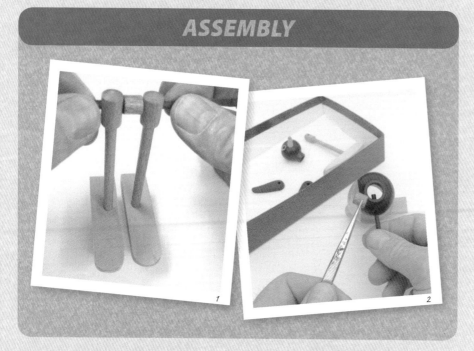

ASSEMBLY

1

2

TUNING UP

Depending how well made your toy is, it should be able to walk on a very slight slope. A little tuning may be necessary and involves hand sanding the felloes to ensure there are no high spots when one is forward and the other is back. Adjust the angle of the slope and make sure the surface is not too slippery. If the toy veers to one side or spins round, then one of the felloes is higher and needs sanding. When you are happy with the action, glue on the arms and the head. Finish with a couple of coats of acrylic lacquer. You may prefer to finish each part before starting to glue. Keep the bottom face of the felloes free of lacquer or polish to stop them slipping.

How it Works

When the toy is placed on a slope and is gently rocked to one side then released, the opposite felloe is lifted clear of the surface and will swing forward down the slope. A board 16in (400mm) long with one end raised ⅜in (10mm) is usually sufficient. The momentum causes the toy to rock back onto this felloe, lifting the other felloe clear and allowing this one to swing forward. This action keeps repeating until the toy reaches the bottom.

VARIATIONS

The number of variations of this toy are almost endless. If you enjoy painting or carving you can change the head to produce almost any character you wish.

The alternatives shown here are a painted penguin and a painted clown, both made from pear wood (*Pyrus communis*) and a baby version made from bubinga (*Guibourtia demeusei*) and boxwood (*Buxus sempervirens*).

That's all for now folks!
Now you are ready for anything!

ABOUT THE AUTHOR

Chris Reid started turning wood as a hobby back in 1957 when he acquired his first lathe. After leaving school, he studied Mechanical and Electrical Engineering, qualifying in 1963. A number of years in product design for various companies followed. Then in 1972, he took a complete change in direction and joined the fire brigade. Woodturning continued to remain a firm interest.

Chris retired from the Fire Service in 1997 and quickly set about organizing his workshop so he could return to the fun of woodturning. The toys in this book came about from having three grandchildren who all enjoy helping him to make things.

His other interests include watercolour painting, messing about in boats, old cars (he has a cherished Morris Minor) and making furniture.

ACKNOWLEDGEMENTS

Writing and publishing a book of this nature is not possible by one person alone, however accomplished. There are a great many people who have contributed their time, talent and knowledge to make this book a reality. To mention them all here is not possible.

Yet I would like to thank Colin Simpson, ex Editor of *Woodturning* magazine, who may be surprised to learn that he was the one who first sowed the seed that encouraged me to write this book.

I could not have managed without the team at GMC Publications.

Thanks to Anthony Bailey for his time and patience in teaching me photography skills and for his professional photography in the book.

I am indebted to Mark Bentley for his skill and courage in taking on the job of Editor. I also owe a particular debt to Beth Wicks, who took over this role and collated the work into one cohesive volume.

Thanks also to Gilda Pacitti for her contribution as Managing Art Editor and for her encouragement and suggestions.

The layout and design are inspired, for that I thank Rebecca Mothersole and Chris and Jane Lanaway.

I am most grateful to Mark Baker, current Editor of *Woodturning* magazine, and Jonathan Bailey, Associate Publisher, for their encouragement and support.

I must also mention and thank my team of toy testers Dean, Dana and Nicholas.

Last but not least, love and thanks to my wife Barbara, who has always been a great support and friend.

Index

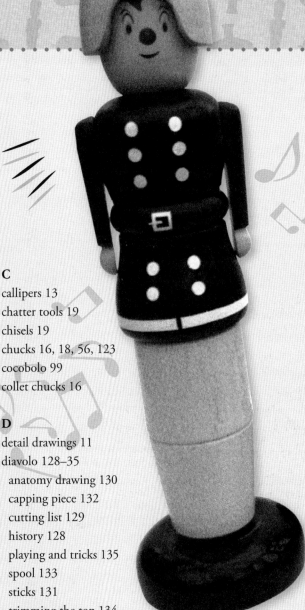

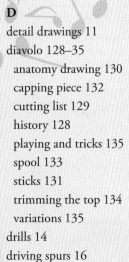